I Love My Boss

& 969 Other Business Jokes

Gene Perret

 Sterling Publishing Co., Inc. New York

to
the coworkers
at 6901
who encouraged
my comedy career

Library of Congress Cataloging-in-Publication Data

Perret, Gene.
    I love my boss & 969 other business jokes   / by Gene Perret.
       p.   cm.
    Includes index.
    ISBN 0-8069-8758-8
    1. Business—Humor.   I. Title.   II. Title: I love my boss and 969
other business jokes.
PN6231.B85P48   1993
818'.5402—dc20   93-13961
                                                         CIP

10 9 8 7 6 5 4 3 2 1

Published by Sterling Publishing Company, Inc.
387 Park Avenue South, New York, N.Y. 10016
© 1993 by Gene Perret
Distributed in Canada by Sterling Publishing
% Canadian Manda Group, P.O. Box 920, Station U
Toronto, Ontario, Canada M8Z 5P9
Distributed in Great Britain and Europe by Cassell PLC
Villiers House, 41/47 Strand, London WC2N 5JE, England
Distributed in Australia by Capricorn Link Ltd.
P.O. Box 665, Lane Cove, NSW 2066
Manufactured in the United States of America
All rights reserved

Sterling ISBN 0-8069-8758-8

CONTENTS

Introduction 10

TIP #1: Use humor to get your message across . . . 11

Unaccustomed As I Am . . .

Playful Introductions. 13
Playful Acceptances of Good Introductions 14
Playful Acceptances—Playfully Bad Introductions. . 15

TIP #2: Humor is not only jokes. 16

Getting There Is Half the Problem

Getting Up in the Morning 17
Monday Morning Blahs. 18

TIP #3: Keep your humor dignified 20

Commuting to Work. 21
Parking Problems 22

TIP #4: Remember your purpose. 23

It's a Mess, but It's My Mess

Messy Desk. 24
Office Coffee. 26

TIP #5: One anecdote can have many
applications. 27

Filing System. 28
Gloomy Offices 29

TIP #6: Use humor sparingly. 31

The Way We Do Business

Business Ethics 32
Customers and Clients. 33

TIP #7: Anybody can tell a joke 34

Committees. 35
Meetings. 36

TIP #8: Put yourself into your humor 37

Memos 38

Scheduling 39

TIP #9: Be conversational 41

Office Security. 42
The Suggestion Box. 43

The Beloved Boss

Stupid Boss. 45
Grouchy Boss 47

TIP #10: Be economical in telling your joke. 49

Forgetful Boss. 49
Cheap Boss. 51

TIP #11: Work at your humor 52

Unlikable Boss 54
You Know Your Boss Hates Your Guts When. . . . 55

Newfangled Technology

Computers 57

TIP #12: Know the ending of your joke. 58

Voice Mail 59

Car Phones 61

TIP #13: Tell your story slowly and clearly 62

Beepers 63
Copying Machines 65

TIP #14: Timing is listening to your audience 67

Fax Machines 67
Vending Machines 69

TIP #15: Laugh at your own jokes? 71

I Love My Coworkers

Secretaries 72
Lazy Coworkers 73

TIP #16: Hear your stories as your listeners will
hear them 74

Absenteeism 75
Lateness 76

TIP #17: Let them know when to laugh 78

Petty Office Thievery 79
Annoying Coworkers 80
Backstabbing 82

TIP #18: Have fun with your mistakes 83

Smokers and Nonsmokers 84

Every Office Has 'Em

Office Collections 86

TIP #19: Build your own humor file 87

Office Rumors 88

The Office Don Juan 89

Office Fun

Business Lunches. 91
Brown Baggers 93

TIP #20: Research your own material 95

The Office Party 95
Briefcases 97

TIP #21: Use proven humor 99

Things You'll Seldom Overhear Around the
Water Cooler 100

Fasten Your Seat Belt

Business Travel 101
Hotels and Motels. 103

TIP #22: How to make a story your own 105

Conventions 105
Expense Accounts 107

TIP #23: Hit your audience right between
the eyes. 108

Take the Money and Run

Payday 109
Payroll Deductions 110
You Know It's Time to Ask for a Raise When. . . 111

TIP #24: Don't announce your jokes. 112

Budgets. 113

Job-Related Stress 114
You Know You Hate Your Job When 115

TIP #25: Don't do what you can't do 117

T.G.I.F.. 117
Vacation 119

TIP #26: Where do the jokes go? 121

Retirement 121
Pink Slips 123

TIP #27: Humor to avoid 124

Index 126

Introduction

In 1992, President George Bush was struggling to be re-elected. His major opponents were Bill Clinton and Ross Perot. The candidates debated each other three times within one week's time, and their running mates debated once.

In listening to the post-debate analyses by the newscasters and political experts, the quotes I heard most often were the witty, humorous, pithy one-liners. Ross Perot said, "They're right. I don't have any experience at running up a $4 trillion debt." His running mate, Jim Stockdale, scored points by interrupting a heated exchange between Messrs. Quayle and Gore with: "I think the Americans are seeing why this country is in gridlock."

The lighthearted, meaningful statements are heard, understood, and remembered by the listeners. They get the message across.

Humor is a powerful tool in any speaker's arsenal. Used wisely, well, and at the right time and place, humor is a powerful communications device.

If presidential candidates can use it to their advantage in their multi-million-dollar campaigns, you can use it to accomplish your goals.

Use humor to get your message across

Stephen Douglas once said this about the humor of his political adversary, Abraham Lincoln: "Every one of his stories seems like a whack upon my back. Nothing else—not any of his arguments or any of his replies to my questions—disturbs me. But when he begins to tell a story, I feel that I am to be overmatched." That's pretty powerful.

You can use a touch of humor to benefit almost any business presentation. "A touch," meaning that the humor should complement the central message, not overwhelm it.

Humor is important because it adds stature to the speaker. Often you hear book titles like *The Wit and Wisdom of So-and-So* because the two are closely aligned. Wit implies wisdom; wisdom implies wit. The two go hand-in-hand, and listeners recognize this.

When an audience hears a speaker who knows enough about the subject to extract the intrinsic humor from it, they know this is a speaker worth listening to. When listeners hear a person who can sense the humor in a topic, they know the person can also sense the *reality* of that topic. A well-rounded sense of humor indicates a sense of balance, too.

When people hear solid, incisive, knowledgeable wit, they respect that speaker.

Humor can entice an audience into listening. Even the most worthwhile message can become wearying for listeners. Even though the speaker is at the podium doing all of the talking, the listeners are working, too. They're absorbing, evaluating, paying attention. It's work. It's tiring. A well-placed chuckle can revitalize them. It can make them perk up and pay attention again.

I've watched audiences at business conventions listening to several speakers. I've seen their heads droop and their attention wander. I've seen them slouch in their seats and abandon their note-taking. Then I've watched as a masterful speaker threw them a couple of comedic gems. They perk up; they listen. They don't want to miss any of the laughs, the refreshing bons mots.

The judicious use of humor can prepare an audience for the salient points of your message. It can refresh their minds, get their attention, and force them to listen to what you want them to hear.

Humor helps listeners remember important features of your presentation. Most books or courses on memory recommend outlandish, bizarre images to help you remember. The zanier the mental picture you create, the easier it is to remember. For instance, if you want to remember the numbers 1245. You might say to yourself, "Let's see . . . there were 12 apostles, so I'll picture the apostles in my mind. Then I'll think of Colt-45's, six-shooters to remember the second half of the number." Now, you picture the apostles in their white robes with gun belts strapped around their waists, shooting off their six-shooters the way cowboys did when they had a wild night in town. This goofy picture should stay in your mind awhile and remind you of the number 1245.

Comedy is a picture-oriented phenomenon, too. Most good jokes create a vivid image in the listener's mind. The image may be different for each listener, but it's usually memorable.

When a speaker couples an important point with a funny, graphic image—even if it's just a short, humorous quote—it marries that image with the message and makes it easier for the listener to remember.

If you can get an audience to respect you, to listen to you, and to remember what you say, you can't ask for too much more. The wise use of humor can do that for you.

Unaccustomed As I Am . . .

♦ Playful Introductions

Our next speaker not only needs no introduction, he doesn't really deserve one.

* * *

Some of you may have heard our next speaker before. We ask that you stay for the presentation anyway.

* * *

I've personally called our next speaker four or five times to ask him if he could be with us tonight. He finally accepted the charges.

* * *

You've heard it said that "the next speaker needs no introduction." That's definitely not true in this case.

. . . Believe me, our next speaker needs all the help he can get.

* * *

I asked our next speaker how he would like to be introduced. He said, "Just tell the truth about me." Well, I couldn't do that to him . . .

* * *

It's difficult to say everything about our next speaker in the one or two minutes allotted to me. To say all the good things I can about this person would take . . . oh . . . three or four minutes.

* * *

I've been allotted one or two minutes to say all the good things I can about our next speaker. I'll try to stretch it out.

* * *

Many, many people have recommended this next speaker to us . . . all members of his own family.

* * *

We've all heard an awful lot about our next speaker. He assures us, though, that none of it is true.

As you know, we traditionally have fine speakers at this event. This evening, for something different . . .

* * *

Our speaker tonight said, "Please give me a very simple introduction." He wanted it to match his speech.

* * *

I could give our speaker tonight a flowery, glowing introduction listing many accomplishments, prestigious awards, his impeccable character and unquestioned ability, but I'm not going to do that. You might not recognize him.

* * *

Our next speaker needs no introduction. It wouldn't help.

* * *

I could deliver an introduction that tells you what a charming and intelligent person our next speaker is, listing all his glowing accomplishments, and telling you what an entertaining and enlightening speaker he is. But I'm not going to do that. I'd rather deliver the introduction I wrote than the one he did.

* * *

Our next speaker has a list of credits as long as your arm. It must have taken him years to make them up.

* * *

We've received hundreds of letters asking us to have this next person as our speaker. Now I'd like you to meet the man who wrote all those letters . . .

◆ Playful Acceptances of Playfully Good Introductions

You're introduction was not only complimentary, but also extremely eloquent. You had me believing most of it, and I know better.

* * *

What a glowing introduction! I'd like to take you along the next time I have to face a tax audit.

That introduction was so nice, I wish now I had prepared a better speech.

* * *

That introduction was so gracious that it makes me feel humble. But I'll get over it before I finish my remarks.

* * *

What a gracious and eloquent introduction. I wish they'd allowed more time for your introduction and less time for my speech.

* * *

What a glorious introduction. Even I can't wait now to hear what I have to say.

. . . And I've heard most of it before.

* * *

Your introduction was extremely generous. If I had known I was going to be that good I would have charged more.

* * *

That introduction was so gracious, you were more than halfway through it before I realized you were talking about me.

* * *

What a fantastic introduction. That's one of the advantages of being introduced by someone who has never heard you speak before.

♦ Playful Acceptances—Playfully Bad Introductions

Sometimes I wish my talk were as good as the introduction I receive. Tonight, obviously, I don't have that concern.

* * *

They asked me who I would like to introduce me tonight and I said, "Oh, you can get just about anybody." So that's who they got.

As a speaker, I've had good introductions and I've had bad ones. This is the first time I've ever had a combination of the two.

. . . This one was good and bad.

* * *

They asked me who I would like to have introduce me this evening and I told them. I'm sorry now that they couldn't get my first, second, or third recommendations.

* * *

They asked me who I would like to have introduce me this evening and I told them. I'm kind of sorry now I just didn't leave it to chance.

* * *

They say sometimes that a speaker needs no introduction. They also say that sometimes after he gets one, he wishes he hadn't.

☞ T I P # 2

Humor is not only jokes

When most of us think of humor or comedy we think of jokes, either one-liners or anecdotes. It's not always words, though. One of the biggest jokes I can remember in my television writing was a man who just turned to another person and shrugged. No words were spoken; none were needed. The gesture, in context, was funny.

Humor is an attitude. You can bring a delightful sense of humor to your presentations without feeling awkward telling jokes you're not sure of or recounting anecdotes that you might be uncomfortable with.

The secret is not to take yourself, your message, or your audience too seriously. The key word is *too*. Certainly you should be listened to, your message heard, and your audience respected . . . but not blown out of proportion.

I once saw a map of the universe. The earth was so tiny it couldn't even be seen, but there was an arrow pointing to its general location and a block of type that read: "You are here."

Keep that sense of perspective in your talk and you'll keep a sense of humor.

Getting There Is Half the Problem

◆ *Getting Up in the Morning*

The worst part about morning is that it comes so early in the day.

* * *

The toughest work we do all day is opening our eyes in the morning.

* * *

I begin every morning with a prayer. I pray that I can go back to sleep again.

* * *

Getting up and going to work is terrible. Staying in bed and going to work probably wouldn't be too bad.

* * *

I never understood that saying "You're going to hate yourself in the morning." I generally hate *everything* in the morning.

* * *

They say the early bird catches the worm. It serves the worm right for being up that early.

* * *

My dad used to preach to me with: "The early bird catches the worm." I didn't want to make Dad feel bad, but a worm's not much of an incentive for getting out of a warm, cozy bed.

My grandfather boasted that every day of his life he got up with the roosters. That's probably because Grandmom made him sleep in the chicken coop.

* * *

My grandfather boasted that every day of his life he got up with the roosters. I don't know if Grandpop knew it or not, but the roosters used to go back to sleep again.

* * *

Why would anybody in his right mind want to get up with the roosters? Unless you're dating a chicken . . .

* * *

I don't know why it is, but whenever my alarm goes off I always want five more minutes of sleep. And going to bed five minutes earlier the night before doesn't help.

* * *

Whoever invented the alarm clock should be sentenced to be shot at dawn. His only hope then would be that the firing squad would oversleep.

* * *

I enjoy hating my alarm clock. There's only one drawback: I have to be awake to do it properly.

* * *

The first thing you should do in the morning is splash cold water on your face, or on the face of the person who woke you up.

* * *

I can't do anything in the morning until I've had a cup of coffee and a shower. By then I'm ready to go back to bed again.

* * *

To me, naps only have one failing: You have to be awake to take them.

◆ Monday Morning Blahs

If the days of the week were the Seven Dwarfs, Monday would be Grumpy.

The worst thing about Monday is that it's followed by Tuesday, Wednesday, Thursday, and Friday.

* * *

What we call the Monday Morning Blahs are really the Friday, Saturday, and Sunday After-Effects.

* * *

About the only thing that snaps me out of the Monday Morning Blahs is Tuesday.

* * *

Monday is "Back to Work" day. Well, it's "Show Up at the Office" day. Not much work gets done till Tuesday.

* * *

Whoever invented the modern-day calendar was a sadist. It has only one Christmas and 52 Mondays.

* * *

Besides, Monday is a terrible thing to put at the end of a weekend.

It's like using the sidewalk to break a fall.

It's like using a safety net made out of barbed wire.

* * *

Every time Monday rolls around I know how Dr. Jekyll felt whenever Mr. Hyde made his appearance.

* * *

When I was a kid I never thought the carnival rides lasted long enough. Now as an adult, I feel that way about weekends.

* * *

Monday wouldn't be so bad if it would start when we wanted it to instead of when the alarm clock goes off.

* * *

I don't know why some people call it "Blue Monday." When my alarm goes off I see red.

* * *

My alarm clock rings four days of the work week. On Monday morning, it doesn't ring; it kicks me in the teeth.

Some people don't mind Monday too much. To them it's just continuing their day of rest on company time.

*   *   *

Monday is a rough day not only because it follows the weekend so closely, but also because it's so far away from payday.

Keep your humor dignified

Bob Hope says about his brief boxing career as a young man: "I put the 'PU' in 'pugilism.'"

Will Rogers responded when asked about his political affiliation: "I belong to no organized political party. I'm a Democrat."

When reporters asked John Kennedy about the closeness of his election victory over Richard Nixon, he said: "My daddy didn't want to pay for a landslide."

Abraham Lincoln once received a dispatch from General Joe Hooker that was signed "Headquarters in the saddle." Lincoln said, "The trouble with Hooker is that he's got his headquarters where his hindquarters ought to be."

These were all funny men. Hope has dined with kings, queens, and world leaders from many nations. Rogers was asked to run for president. Kennedy and Lincoln, of course, were presidents. They were all well-respected figures.

Humor and dignity do mix. Humor and dignity *should* mix.

Keep in mind that any comedy material you incorporate into your presentations (and the people we've mentioned above incorporated much humor into all their communications) should always be dignified.

Humor can be a part of your life without threatening your status in any way.

◆ *Commuting to Work*

"Commuting" today is a four-letter word, and then some.

*   *   *

Driving to and from work can be a peaceful time, if you can close your eyes to the stresses of the world and the obscene gestures of your fellow motorists.

*   *   *

Drivers today are getting terrible. Years ago they used to let me cut them off, now they don't.

*   *   *

A highway jammed with cars is really not too much of a problem in today's world. The problem is that all of the cars have drivers in them.

*   *   *

The problem with today's traffic is that everyone is in such a terrible hurry to get where they really don't want to go.

*   *   *

There's just too much traffic. Years ago you could get where you were going on time. Nowadays, you're lucky if you can get there before the next payment on your car is due.

*   *   *

Traffic today is getting terrible. I don't know where all the cars are coming from, but I know they're all going the same place I am.

*   *   *

Traffic is horrendous nowadays. The other day I was 20 minutes late getting to the office . . . and I work at home.

*   *   *

The other day on the freeway I was in traffic behind two people who smooched all the way home. He was in a white Ford and she was in a blue Chevrolet.

*   *   *

There's a lot of stress on today's highways. Recent surveys have revealed that 60 percent of steering wheels have teeth marks in them.

It used to be that the early bird caught the worm. Not anymore, because the early bird is probably held up in traffic.

* * *

Traffic is so congested nowadays they're building all the new highways without on-ramps. There's no room for any new people.

* * *

I won't say there's a lot of traffic on today's roads, but a pleasant ride to the office nowadays is one in which you finish in the same car you started with.

* * *

I used ride-sharing to get to the office this morning. I didn't mean to. I just locked bumpers with the car ahead of me.

* * *

Cars are just jammed on the highways today. I pushed in my cigarette lighter and blew up the car in front of me.

◆ Parking Problems

Parking is a big problem in the business world . . . whether you have a car or not.

* * *

A good parking space is a sure sign of status within the company. My house is closer to the office than my parking space.

. . . After work, it's easier for me to walk home and have my wife drive me to my car.

* * *

I hate to tell you how far my assigned parking space is from the building, but it comes with a travel agent.

* * *

My parking space is so far away that when I leave my car and walk to the office, I pass my house.

* * *

My parking space is so far away from the office that by the time I get to my car after work, I'm halfway home.

If my parking space were any further away from the building, I'd have to carry both a driver's license and a passport.

* * *

I have such a long walk to and from my parking space that I put more mileage on my shoes each year than on my car.

* * *

I'm so low on the company hierarchy, they gave me a great assigned parking space. They know I don't make enough money to afford a car.

* * *

I have a pretty good parking space now. My last performance evaluation was so low, I'm allowed to park in the handicapped zone.

* * *

My assigned parking space is so bad, if they arranged them alphabetically I'd still be about a half a block further away then Mr. Zzyzzenflaus.

* * *

The next best thing to a good assigned parking space is a secretary who's willing to run outside every two hours to put another quarter in the meter.

* * *

I have a *pretty good* corporate parking space. It's convenient because it's very close to the building. It's inconvenient because twice a week the police tow my car away.

* * *

I have a great parking space where I work. I had my name legally changed to "Loading and Unloading Only."

☞ T I P # 4

Remember your purpose

A business speaker has a hidden agenda in using humor. That agenda is: to enhance the presentation and make the message more powerful and readily accepted. Audience laughter is a fringe benefit.

Keep this purpose in mind when you select, write, and present your humor. True, one goal certainly should be to entertain your audience, but the most important one is to help the presentation.

Ask yourself, "Does this material improve my status in the eyes of the audience and make me more worthy of their attention?" "Does it complement my message?" "Does it make my important points more understandable?" "More acceptable?" "Does it help my audience listen to my presentation?" "Does it help them remember it?" "Does it relax and revitalize my listeners so they can pay better attention to what I'm saying?"

If it does those things and gets a chuckle or a smile, it's a good piece of material. If it does those things and gets solid laughter, it's a fantastic piece of material. Be proud of it and use it wisely.

It's a Mess, but It's My Mess

◆ Messy Desk

I cleaned off the top of my desk the other day and found two employees we thought had retired.

* * *

If Stanley had been lost on my desk top, Livingstone would never have found him.

* * *

Some of the paperwork buried on my desk is so old it's written on papyrus.

* * *

There's so much junk piled on top of my desk, it's been condemned by the Board of Health.

Things are piled so precariously high on my desk top, when my secretary comes in to take a letter, he wears a hard hat.

* * *

There's no room for anything more on my desk top. If I want to relax for a minute, I have to lean back in my chair and put my feet up on someone else's desk.

* * *

You've heard of people who collapsed at the office and were found with their heads down on their desks. That can't happen to me. There's no room on my desk top.

* * *

My boss said, "Why don't you get rid of some of the stuff on the top of your desk?" If I do that, the other stuff will fall over.

* * *

My desk top has gotten so bad I'm not allowed to clean it anymore. My doctor said, "No heavy lifting."

* * *

I can't find anything on my desk top, which is not really a problem until the phone rings.

* * *

It's well known around the office that anything that touches my desk top is immediately lost. Which at least keeps people from sitting on the edge of my desk.

* * *

Anything that reaches my desk stops there forever. That's because my "out" basket has been hopelessly lost for the past seven years.

* * *

I'll give you an idea what the top of my desk looks like. Have you seen a recent aerial photo of Beirut?

* * *

My desk top looks like a landfill with coffee stain rings.

* * *

I have so much junk piled on my desk top that, to tell the truth, I'm not even sure there's a desk under it.

♦ Office Coffee

We have a rule in our office: The first one to arrive in the morning makes the coffee. Everyone after that complains about it.

* * *

Sometimes the coffee in our office is pretty bad. The author of *Final Exit* asked if he could include the recipe.

* * *

We have two kinds of people working in our office: those who don't drink coffee, and those who do and lived to tell about it.

* * *

One of our employees called and said, "I'm calling in sick today; I drank the coffee yesterday."

* * *

Most people in our office start the day with a cup of coffee. If they can get by that, facing the boss is a pushover.

* * *

The coffee in our office leaves an after taste . . . forever after.

* * *

I asked one coworker in our office how he liked his coffee. He said, "Black . . . or whatever color it turned out today."

* * *

Some businesses demand that you wear a hard hat when you go out into the factory. Ours demands you wear a hard hat when you drink the coffee.

* * *

We never waste coffee in our office. What we don't drink we send to NASA as rocket fuel.

* * *

No one ever washes the coffeepot in our office. We've never found a detergent that's equal to the task.

* * *

We tried to scrub the coffeepot once and people found the soapy water preferable to the coffee.

We have to replace the coffeepot in our office about once a month. It keeps wearing out . . . from the inside.

* * *

The people in our office make three different types of coffee—strong, extra-strong, and "Oh, no, it set off the automatic sprinkler system again."

* * *

A few people in our office pour a cup of coffee in the morning. By mid-afternoon they can spread it on a cracker.

* * *

Sometimes the coffee in our office is so strong you can have it either by the cup or by the scoop.

* * *

We have occasions where people have dropped the coffeepot and it shattered, but the coffee remained intact.

* * *

Sometimes our coffee is so strong it can make your hair stand on end . . . even on the people who aren't having any.

* * *

The coffee in our office is so strong, instead of taking it with cream, some people take it with Maalox®.

* * *

We once had a small fire in our office. The firemen quickly put it out, but three of them had to be treated for coffee inhalation.

* * *

Many secretaries nowadays belong to the M.Y.O.C. union—Make Your Own Coffee.

☞ TIP #5

One anecdote can have many applications

I sometimes tell the story about how my daughter in kindergarten asked me to help her with a school recital she had to give. I suggested that since I wrote for some pretty famous people, I might be able to write something for her that was funny, different, and original. She said, "Well, Dad, this is in front of the whole school. I'd rather it be good."

That line can be used to illustrate humility, or it can show an audience the value of being prepared. It can also be used as an example of keeping an open mind, and listening to everyone's suggestions because sometimes wisdom comes from the least expected sources. Additionally, it can teach an audience the value of not settling for anything less than their best. One story can have that many uses.

Good snippets of humor are valuable. They're rare. When you have a workable quote, story, or anecdote you can use it for varied purposes. Rather than seek out a new piece of material for each point you want to emphasize, utilize the good material you already have.

Be inventive in finding other applications for your humor. One story is not locked into one message. Many others may be hidden within it. Find those other messages and your repertoire of humor will expand tremendously.

◆ *Filing System*

My secretary has a very simple filing system. Everything goes under "L" for "Lost."

. . . Either there or under "S" for "Still Lost."

I said, "If you happen to find something, where do you file it?" He said, "Under 'W' for 'Will Be Lost Again.' "

I asked, "Don't you have a drawer marked 'F'?" He said, "Of course. That stands for 'Forget It.' "

* * *

My secretary loses everything I ask him to find. Every time I try to fire him, I can't find him.

. . . He hides in the file cabinet.

. . . Under "G" for "Hiding."

My secretary's filing system works fine 95% of the time. The only time it doesn't work is when you want to find something.

* * *

My secretary is so adept at losing things he saves the office money. We don't have to buy a paper shredder.

* * *

My secretary firmly believes there's a place for every-thing—unfortunately, he has no idea where that is.

* * *

My secretary devised his own filing system, which he claims will make him a lot of money. It already has. Every time I ask him to find something, I have to pay him overtime.

* * *

My secretary's busy right now writing a dictionary where the words aren't listed in alphabetical order. They're listed by height.

* * *

My secretary has written a book about his filing system. It's called "Gone With the Wind."

* * *

The rule of thumb in my office is: If you think you're going to need something again, sew it inside your underwear.

* * *

My secretary has a one-drawer filing system. Things he can't find, he files under "L" for "Lost"; things he can find, he files under "L" for "Lucky."

◆ Gloomy Offices

My office is so dank and dreary it doesn't have a carpet on the floor. It's covered with moss.

* * *

My office is so dreary it's a good thing it doesn't have a window. It would be too depressing for outsiders looking in.

Lower-level executives get buried in the bowels of the building. My office doesn't have a watercooler. It's fed by an underwater spring.

*   *   *

My office is so low in the building, when I leave at night I have to take the "up" elevator to reach the parking lot.

*   *   *

When the mail boy comes to our floor, he wears a miner's cap with a light on it.

*   *   *

Mine is a gloomy office. Even the Muzak® in there only plays funeral dirges.

*   *   *

My office is so gloomy it's cryptlike. You should always look alive when you're at work, but in my office that seems strangely inappropriate.

*   *   *

I'll give you an idea of the size of my office. Have you ever been in a 747? Well, my office is about the size of one over-head bin.

*   *   *

My office is so small that when visitors come in, they have to leave their briefcases outside.

*   *   *

If my office were a parking space it would be marked "Compact Cars Only."

*   *   *

My office is so small that once they put the desk in, there was no room for me.

*   *   *

My office is so small it forces me to stay busy. I have to go through yesterday's mail in order to make room for today's.

*   *   *

I can't use the bottom drawer of my filing cabinet. There's not enough room in my office for me to bend over.

My office is so small it's embarrassing. I have to hold my staff meetings in the parking lot.

* * *

My office is so small that when I have lunch at my desk, I have to leave the side dishes outside.

☞ T I P   # 6

Use humor sparingly

Comedians are on stage to entertain. They measure their success by how many laughs they get and how loud those laughs are. Their sole purpose is to make people laugh.

Business speakers are on the podium to enlighten or inspire their listeners. Their primary goal is to get a message across. Humor is a tool for them, not the sole intent.

Comedians should get the biggest laughs they can and strive for as many as possible. Business speakers should use humor sparingly.

A business speaker should use comedy the way a good chef uses salt—season the food to taste. The seasoning should not overpower the natural taste of the food; it should complement and enhance it.

How much is enough? It's hard to say. It's a judgment call you must make. One rule of thumb is: When in doubt, leave it out.

It's much wiser for a business speaker to offend with too little humor than too much. Even the professionals advise, "Always leave 'em laughing." The logic is simple: If they're begging for more, you're a success; if they're tired of you, you're a failure.

The Way We Do Business

◆ *Business Ethics*

Business ethics is nothing more than the Golden Rule dressed up in a suit and tie.

* * *

Business executives should never lie, cheat, or mislead. That's what they have employees for.

* * *

We should all conduct our business lives so that nobody ever has to read the fine print.

* * *

You'll do better in the long run if you keep your shoulder to the wheel rather than your hand in the till.

* * *

Some executives think the Ten Commandments don't apply to business because they were first presented by Moses, who wasn't even a lawyer.

* * *

Some executives think if God wanted business people to follow the Ten Commandments He would have faxed them to us instead of carving them in stone.

* * *

One executive combined ethics with good business sense. He always did what was morally right, but hoped that someone would overrule him.

* * *

Shoplifters hide things under their coats. Unethical business people hide things under their legal departments.

* * *

I knew one businessman who was so corrupt he had to become ambidextrous to keep both sets of books.

* * *

I asked one business associate how things were going. He said, "It depends on which set of books you're reading."

There are good and bad in every profession. Ethics is what enables us to tell them apart.

◆ Customers and Clients

The customer is always right. I like that. It takes the pressure off of me.

* * *

Sometimes I envy undertakers. They only have to deal with the customer once.

* * *

Sometimes I envy doctors. They can tell their customers right to their faces that they're sick.

* * *

Sometimes I envy hookers. They can tell their customers what to do and then charge them for it.

* * *

The customer is *not* always right. Once the check clears, he can be as wrong as the rest of us.

* * *

All of us in business want the customer to come back— hopefully not with the product in his hands.

* * *

There are only three types of customers—cash, check, or credit card.

* * *

Wouldn't it be nice to be able to run a business without customers? But that's like trying to have a doctor run a business without bacteria.

. . . Except that bacteria can be cured.

* * *

Customers do have one thing that all business people admire . . . money.

* * *

Some businesses have clients. Client . . . that's a customer who thinks he's in charge.

A customer pays for what he gets. A client pays for what he thinks he's getting.

* * *

A customer can complain anytime he wants. A client can, too, except that he's paying for the phone call.

* * *

A customer can sometimes buy something that doesn't work. A client usually hires something that doesn't work.

* * *

You have to *give* something to a customer. You don't have to give anything to a client; you just have to *charge* him for it.

☛ T I P # 7

Anybody can tell a joke

Many people quarrel with that statement. They say, "I've tried and I can't tell a joke." I disagree with that. I say anybody can tell a joke provided he picks a good joke and tells it in his own style.

Too many speakers rush into humor. They find a joke— any joke—and then tell it. They don't analyze it to see if it's really funny and if it's appropriate.

The first essential is to find *good* humor—humor that complements your message and is consistent with your message and your speaking style.

The other mistake speakers make is to tell the joke exactly as they heard it. That is, to tell it in someone else's style. You're the speaker now. You have to tell *your* story in *your* style.

Find good, humorous material, become comfortable with it, tell it confidently in you own manner. Do all that and you'll discover that anybody can tell a joke.

♦ Committees

Scarlett O'Hara said, "I'll worry about that tomorrow." She might just as easily have said, "I'll form a committee to look into that."

* * *

Most committees are confusion with a chairman.

* * *

Seventy-two percent of a committee's time is spent deciding when to meet.

* * *

One advantage of serving on a committee is you don't ever have to worry about eating lunch alone.

* * *

A committee is a group of people who can't decide on lunch trying to decide on the solution to a problem.

* * *

A committee is a group of people who will come up with the right answer or a group of people you can blame for the wrong answer.

* * *

Committees always have the same directive: Solve the problem or keep studying it until it goes away.

* * *

One committee had so much trouble finding an answer, they had to appoint another committee to define the question.

* * *

One committee took so long to find a solution, when they finally did, no one could remember what the problem was.

* * *

If at first you don't succeed, appoint a committee. They'll take so long, you'll never have to worry about failing a second time.

♦ Meetings

If my boss has no meetings scheduled for the day, he calls an emergency meeting to find out why.

* * *

Businesspeople love meetings. I know one executive who joined Alcoholics Anonymous, not because he had a drinking problem, but because they held meetings.

* * *

To some executives, the saddest words in the English language are "Meeting adjourned."

* * *

Some executives begin each day by asking, "Should I call a meeting today or should I get some work done?" So they call a meeting to discuss it.

* * *

When an employee doesn't want to do any work he's called shiftless; when the boss doesn't want to do any work, he calls a meeting.

* * *

What's a businessperson's definition of death? When you wake up in the morning and have no meetings to go to.

* * *

A business meeting is a group of people gathered together for one single purpose. They usually have to hold another meeting to find out what it is.

* * *

I asked my boss why he attends so many meetings. He said, "Free coffee."

* * *

Lunch meetings are probably the most productive. It's hard to say something stupid with your mouth full.

* * *

A meeting to a businessperson is like a salt lick to a deer.

"I'm sorry, he's at a meeting" is the business world's equivalent of "Not tonight, dear; I have a headache."

* * *

A business meeting is usually little more than a bull session with a chairperson.

* * *

If all the people who attended meetings were laid end to end, they'd be a lot more comfortable . . . but it would make it harder to take notes.

* * *

If you have something to say at a business meeting, say it. That is, if you can get a word in edgewise between those who don't have anything to say and are saying it.

* * *

Meetings begin by banging the gavel. They should bang the gavel at the middle of the meeting; that's when most people need waking up.

☞ T I P # 8

Put yourself into your humor

One speaker I heard made the comment that humor was composed of two syllables—"you" and "more." It was his way of reminding the listeners to put more of themselves into their humor.

It's a worthwhile message. You have a distinctive style and flair, both as a person and as a speaker. You walk a certain way, talk a certain way, and use your own repertoire of gestures and facial expressions.

It's wrong to abandon these in order to do certain kinds of humor. It's confusing to an audience if you speak like yourself through most of your presentation, but speak like Rodney Dangerfield or Joan Rivers when you do comedy.

Rather than alter your style to fit the humor you're using, alter the material to fit your speaking style.

Woody Allen can't do Bill Cosby's act. Cosby can't do Woody's act, either. Each of them can only do his own style of comedy.

You, too, can only do your brand of humor.

◆ *Memos*

Memo: interoffice junk mail.

* * *

A memo is usually an interoffice communication written by someone who doesn't know to someone who doesn't care to know.

* * *

A memo is usually something uninteresting, about something unimportant, written by someone uninformed, to someone uninvolved.

* * *

The structure of memos is rigid: "From" then "To," followed by the straight line, then the punch line.

* * *

All memos begin with the words "From" and "To." Many of them effectively end there, too.

* * *

A memo lies somewhere between an official document and a perfectly good blank sheet of paper.

* * *

Memos should be short, sweet, and to the point, if any.

* * *

"Put that in a memo" means: "I don't have time to listen to you now, so write it down, and I won't read it later."

* * *

Memo is short for "memorandum," and long for just about everything else.

* * *

In business, anything that's not worth saying is worth writing a memo about.

Many memos are a waste of time with a mailing list attached.

* * *

The problem with many memos is that some things that are better left unsaid should also have been left unwritten.

* * *

The good thing about a memo is that it's a permanent record of your thoughts. That's also the bad thing about it, too.

* * *

Memos lie somewhere below jungle drums as a form of primitive communication.

* * *

If all the memos written in our office in a single day were lined up end to end, they'd be a lot easier to sweep up.

◆ *Scheduling*

My boss has a sign over his desk that reads: "Of course I want it now. If I wanted it tomorrow, I would have given it to you tomorrow."

* * *

Superiors give impossible deadlines. God made the world in six days and on the seventh day He rested. That was only because He was self-employed.

* * *

People in business have learned that the promised date is simply the "due date." Every date thereafter becomes the "overdue date."

* * *

The date a business promises completion is not the date the project is completed. It's just your first warning.

* * *

Where I work, we always give our customers three dates—an estimated completion date, a definite completion date, and a date to call for another estimated completion date.

My boss tells me when he wants a project completed and I tell him how much money I want to earn. We both know we're only kidding.

*   *   *

My boss gave me five days of work and wanted me to complete it in two. I said, "I'll give it to you in three days, but it will take somebody five days to fix it."

*   *   *

My boss wanted the work done in five days. I said 10. He said six. I said eight. We settled on seven.

. . . . I delivered it in 12.

. . . He was delighted with my promptness.

*   *   *

My boss said, "Why do you hand in all your projects late?" I said, "I hand them in on time. You just expect them all early."

*   *   *

I said to my boss, "If I were performing brain surgery on you, would you want me to rush?" He said, "If I let you do the surgery, my brain would be too far gone to be helped, so you could take your time."

*   *   *

My boss wanted a project done on time. He said, "Dependability is the cornerstone of business." I said, "I'm going to be a week late . . . depend on it."

*   *   *

My boss doesn't know what he's doing and he doesn't know what I do. All he knows is when he wants it done.

*   *   *

One coworker claims he has never missed a schedule by more than five working days. When asked when a job will be completed, he simply says, "Friday."

Be conversational

Professional comedy traditionally has a wackiness to it. Baggy pants are the symbol of the burlesque comic. Oversized shoes and a red nose are the trademarks of the clown. Exaggerated takes and affected speech patterns still persist in stand-up comedy today. Comics like to emphasize the joke word, hence the word "*punch* line." It's why comics feel words with a "K" in them are funnier than words without—you can *punch* that sound harder.

Business speakers should resist that tendency, even though they hear the professionals doing it constantly. It's affected. It's unnatural. And unless done well, it can detract from the humor.

Many professional comics stand on the stage in character. They're playing a role. Hiding behind that persona they can speak with wacky inflections and goofy facial contortions. The business speaker stands at the podium as himself or herself. The business speaker's presentation should be conversational.

You want your listeners to believe your message. They first must believe you. It's difficult for them to accept you if you're enunciating words like Rodney Dangerfield, or speaking out of the side of your mouth like Buddy Hackett, or jumping in and out of characters like Robin Williams, or complaining about your neuroses like Richard Lewis.

You're most effective being yourself. Your most powerful speech uses your natural speaking voice, inflections, and gestures.

Talk to your listeners; don't put on a show for them.

♦ Office Security

Security in our building is so lax that the emergency number has an answering machine.

It's quicker to fax your problem to them.

And they respond by UPS.

* * *

It's hard to feel totally secure in a building guarded by a guy named "Pops."

He's older than the Pinkerton Detective Agency.

* * *

Pops is only effective if trouble starts on the ground floor. He gets nauseated when he rides elevators.

* * *

Pops is not much of a deterrent to troublemakers. He's one of the few security guards in the world who carries a gun with training wheels.

* * *

Pops is the only security guard whose snoring is louder than the alarm system.

* * *

For obvious reasons I can't divulge Pops' age, but his social security number is 6.

* * *

Pops gets the name of everyone entering and leaving the building—and then forgets it.

* * *

We have I.D. passes now with our picture on them so the security guard can identify us. I was refused entrance last week. I had my I.D. pass but I left my face at home.

* * *

So long as I look like the photo on my I.D. pass I'm OK, which is silly. Anybody who looks like the picture on my pass should never be allowed to enter any building.

I hate I.D. passes. I don't need anything else hanging from my body that could fall off.

* * *

In our building we have to wear a pass hanging from some part of our clothing. About the only thing that does is keep nude people out of the building.

* * *

You absolutely need an I.D. pass to get into our office. Competence is not required, just an I.D. pass.

* * *

I left my plastic I.D. pass on the dashboard of my car one day and it melted. It ruined the pass, but the photograph improved.

* * *

Our office is protected by four surveillance television cameras and none works. They blend right in with the office staff.

* * *

I don't know why our office needs security. If the competition stole our ideas, they'd be four years behind us.

Besides, our elevators are so slow that whatever the competition stole would be outdated by the time it got to street level.

◆ The Suggestion Box

You know what a suggestion box is—that's limbo for good ideas.

* * *

Our company doesn't pay much attention to employees' ideas. We have a suggestion box that flushes.

* * *

The suggestion box in our office is pretty devious. It's just a slot in the wall that leads directly to the paper shredder.

* * *

The employees' suggestion box is a square little thing with a hole in the top. That also describes quite a few of the employees.

The clearly labeled suggestion box is a labor-saving device for the executive. When an employee has a bright idea, the executive doesn't have to tell him what to do with it.

* * *

The suggestion box is never quite sure what it wants to be—a good place for bad ideas or a bad place for good ideas.

* * *

The employees' suggestion box is only for good ideas. Bad ideas, management can handle on their own.

* * *

The employees' suggestion box is a place where you turn in good ideas so some executive can later claim he thought of them.

* * *

If it weren't for the employees' suggestion box some executives would have no creativity at all.

* * *

Every employee has ideas for the boss. The suggestion box is for the clean ones.

Or at the very least, the physically possible ones.

* * *

Our boss claims he gets an average of 30 suggestions a month and 27 begin with the words "Go take a flying leap . . ."

. . . And 25 of those are written with some sort of indelible venom.

* * *

Our company has a quota. Each employee has to turn in two suggestions each week. Last year I handed in two good ideas and 102 suggestions that they get rid of the suggestion box.

* * *

I turned in one suggestion that saved my company $637.93 a week. They fired me because of it.

The Beloved Boss

◆ *Stupid Boss*

My boss is so stupid, when his mind goes blank it's an improvement.

* * *

When my boss begins a meeting by saying "I've got something on my mind," you know he's lying.

* * *

My boss has the mentality of a child. He doesn't read reports we hand in; he just looks at the pictures.

. . . He doesn't subscribe to the *Wall Street Journal* because it doesn't have a "funnies" page.

* * *

My boss has a mind like a steel trap—which means it's not much good for anything except snaring furry little animals.

* * *

My boss works long hours. Nine to 5 isn't enough time for all the stupid mistakes he makes.

* * *

My boss is so stupid he has to take sick leave to go into heavy thought.

* * *

My boss has had only one creative thought in his life. He thought it was a nightmare.

* * *

My boss claims to have a photographic memory—which means if he has an idea he has to send it out to be developed.

* * *

My boss not only keeps reminding us that he's top man on the totem pole, but he's got the wooden head to back it up.

* * *

Some people think that my boss acts real stupid, but they're wrong. He's not acting.

My boss is so stupid, if you gave him the key to the city, he'd probably lock himself out.

*   *   *

My boss has a brain like Einstein's . . . dead since 1955.

*   *   *

I think the only reason they made my boss an executive was because he was too stupid to learn how to punch the time clock.

*   *   *

When they were giving out brains, my boss thought they said "drains," and said, "Give me one that empties quickly."

*   *   *

When they were giving out brains, my boss thought they said "trains," and said, "Give me one that keeps going around in circles."

*   *   *

People consider my boss well dressed if all the clothes he's wearing are facing in the same direction.

*   *   *

My boss's head actually comes to a point. At masquerade parties he paints his head black and goes as a sharpened pencil.

*   *   *

My boss is so stupid, rumor has it he tried to avoid the draft by getting half undressed and going into a restaurant. The sign in the window said, "No shirt, no service."

*   *   *

My boss's head is so hollow he thinks with an echo.

*   *   *

My boss almost choked to death one time. He thought he could eat hot red peppers because he's color blind.

*   *   *

During a power outage in our office building my boss was stuck for three hours—on the escalator.

My boss is so stupid he once locked himself out of his car. It took him two hours to get it unlocked and let his family out.

*   *   *

My boss is so stupid his lucky number is "blue."

*   *   *

My boss reads mystery novels backwards. He knows who did it, but he doesn't know what they did.

*   *   *

My boss is so stupid, when he gets amnesia, he actually gets smarter.

*   *   *

My boss is so stupid he doesn't know a spreadsheet from spaghetti and meatballs. Don't ever let him order dinner for you.

*   *   *

My boss is so stupid, if he fell out an office window, he'd have to ask directions to find out which way to fall.

◆ Grouchy Boss

My boss is a real grouch. Even when he calls you into his office for a raise, nobody wants to go.

*   *   *

Nobody likes my boss. He told us one day that the door to his office is always open . . . so we all closed ours.

*   *   *

We call our boss by the initials B.P. That's because he has the personality of the Bubonic Plague.

*   *   *

My boss is a hard-nosed executive. He has a black belt in management.

*   *   *

If my boss were suddenly made the warden of a Turkish prison, he would consider it a lateral move.

My boss is a real grouch. Every time he walks by the coffee machine, the milk curdles.

*   *   *

My boss came up the hard way—without a personality.

*   *   *

My boss's last secretary hated him so much that he quit and went back to his old job—training pit bulls.

*   *   *

My boss is a tough executive. He has all the tact and diplomacy of a firing squad.

*   *   *

My boss is such a grouch that whenever you're called into his office you're entitled to a cigarette and a blindfold.

*   *   *

My boss is always in a foul mood. On the corporate organizational chart, his picture is the one with a black cloud over it.

*   *   *

My boss is such a grouch, he can make a roomful of people happy just by going out the door. Of course, if he goes out the window, that makes them even happier still.

*   *   *

My boss has a terrible personality. Some people in the office say that's because he sits on it all day.

*   *   *

The boss rules our department with an iron fist. We just can't wait till he gets a case of jock itch.

*   *   *

If my boss's personality were an apartment building, he'd be a slumlord.

*   *   *

I won't say my boss is tough, but if you took a day off to be a pallbearer, he'd ask for a note from the deceased.

Be economical in telling your joke

There's a certain economy to telling a joke. Let me use a near-perfect joke to illustrate:

"Why do firemen wear red suspenders?"
"To hold their pants up."

Now let me tell that same joke two other ways:

"Why do firemen wear suspenders?"
"To hold their pants up."

and:

"Why do firemen wear red suspenders?"
"Because red suspenders hold their pants up much better than blue or yellow or green suspenders."

The second and third telling ruin the joke, don't they? Why? Well, let's study the logic of the original joke. In the question, the emphasis is on the word "red." But the answer emphasizes the word "suspenders." Basically, that's the humor of the joke.

In the second telling, omitting the word "red" destroys the misdirection of the gag. It doesn't give the audience enough information.

In the third telling, stressing the different colors in the reply also destroys the intent of the joke. It supplies too much information to the listeners.

That, in a nutshell, is the economy of telling a joke. Shakespeare admonished, "Brevity is the soul of wit." That means, tell the audience all that they need to know to appreciate the joke, but not so much that you destroy the essence of the humor.

◆ *Forgetful Boss*

My boss sometimes remembers everything. That's because he's so forgetful, he often forgets he's forgetful.

My boss is very thoughtful. The two questions he asks his employees most often are: "What are you working on?" and "Who are you?"

* * *

My boss is so forgetful he works a lot of overtime. It's easier than trying to remember where he parked his car.

* * *

My forgetful boss once bawled me out for not having an important project completed.

He said, "Now when can you hand it in?"
I said, "I handed it in last Wednesday."
He said, "You handed what in?"

* * *

My boss is always forgetting important engagements. He has two secretaries—one to make appointments and one to write apologies.

* * *

My boss is very forgetful. He tells all new employees, "I have two hard-and-fast rules. First, I don't tolerate dumb mistakes, and second, I won't tolerate dumb mistakes."

* * *

My boss actually thinks he has a good memory. That's because he keeps forgetting things he didn't remember.

* * *

My boss has a terrible memory. Have you ever seen those signs that say, "You are here"? They're put there just for him.

For him, those signs should say, "You are here. Don't move, and someone will come and get you."

* * *

My boss is very forgetful. Many times he's worn two different colored socks to work. No shoes—just two different colored socks.

* * *

My boss is the most forgetful person I've ever met. He's always losing pencils . . . while he's writing.

Each year my boss gives a plaque to his outstanding employee. It's engraved: "For doing something good, but I can't remember what."

* * *

My boss is so forgetful that he has his name painted on his office door . . . on the inside.

* * *

Some people can't remember faces. My boss can't remember entire bodies.

* * *

My boss is very slim. He keeps forgetting to eat his lunch.

◆ Cheap Boss

My boss is so cheap, the only way you can get him to pick up a check is to put a dime under it.

* * *

Anytime you eat with my boss it's a business lunch, because when the check comes, he gives you the business.

* * *

My boss is so cheap, his wallet is marked "For Deposits Only."

* * *

My boss never spends anything. When he buys a new wallet he immediately coats the inside of it with Krazy Glue®.

* * *

They say crime doesn't pay. It will if it ever goes to lunch with my boss.

* * *

My boss is a very religious man. He figures as long as his hands are folded in prayer, they won't be tempted to reach into his pocket.

* * *

Even if my boss invites you to his house for dinner, you have to bring your own food.

He buys one Christmas card every year and then sends it out in the form of a chain letter.

. . . If you break the chain, you have a lousy New Year.

* * *

If you have a meeting in my boss's office, his secretary says, "Would anybody care to purchase a cup of coffee?"

* * *

My boss is very frugal with office supplies. If you want to get a legal pad, you have to get a lawyer to co-sign for you.

* * *

My boss is so cheap, he wants us to write letters on both sides of the paper—even if they're going to different people.

* * *

My boss is so cheap, if you take a client to lunch, he expects you to turn in a receipt and a doggie bag.

* * *

My boss is so cheap, he goes over every expense account with a fine-tooth comb—and it's a borrowed comb.

* * *

My boss wants to know where heaven is, because when he dies and goes there he wants to know how many frequent flyer miles he'll get.

* * *

They say, "You can't take it with you." If that's true, my boss is coming back for it.

☞ *TIP #11*

Work at your humor

Good humor should appear effortless. The professional comedians we see on television, in movies, and in theaters make their performances look easy. Their comedy appears natural, spontaneous. It isn't.

I've worked with enough legendary humorists to know they work hard on both their material and their delivery.

Most of them are almost fanatical about their preparation. At rehearsals they want to know exactly where to stand, which camera will be operating as they speak, where the other performers will be and what they'll be doing. They want to know about the sound system, the lighting. They're concerned about every tiny detail of their presentation. They realize that detailed preparation makes the performance seem effortless.

This can be misleading, though. We see an effortless performance and assume that comedy should always be spontaneous. Comedy requires work.

Speakers should always work hard on their humor. It may be a small part of your speech, but it is an important part. It is effective when done well, and to be done well it deserves as much or more effort as the rest of your presentation.

First, work hard on your research, which material you'll use. Find jokes, stories, or quotes that convey your ideas accurately. Not just any "funny" story should do, only the correct one—the one that says exactly what you want to say.

The material you select should be tasteful and should reflect your own philosophy.

Second, you should position it correctly in your speech. A business speaker's humor is there to reinforce a message, illustrate a point, or make an item more memorable. Think about that when placing humor into your presentation. What is the purpose of your story, and how does it best accomplish that purpose?

Third, work on your delivery. Humor is more than material. It's solid material combined with effective presentation. Reword your anecdote so it sounds more like you. Practice saying it aloud until you're comfortable hearing yourself say it. Tell it to friends, trying different phrasing and inflection so you can determine for yourself which delivery is most effective.

Effort beforehand makes your humor easy once you get to the dais.

♦ Unlikable Boss

My boss is not a likable guy. More people like tainted tuna fish than like him.

*   *   *

Nobody likes my boss. When he was a kid, his parents liked his imaginary friend more than they liked him.

*   *   *

My boss is not a very likable guy. His best friend in the whole world is an acquaintance who just tolerates him.

*   *   *

When my boss got married, his best man was rented along with the tuxedos.

*   *   *

Nobody likes my boss. He once called the suicide hot line and the person who answered pretended to be the maid.

*   *   *

No one in the office even likes to talk to my boss. Out of politeness they'll say, "How're you doing?" but they quickly add, "You don't have to answer me now."

*   *   *

Our boss has no friends in the office. At the company picnic he hangs around with the ants.

*   *   *

Our boss is so disliked, instead of a secretary he has a food taster.

. . . In fact, he's had five of them. The first four died suddenly.

*   *   *

The boss always said he didn't take this job to win a popularity contest. But it would have been nice if he could have gotten at least *one* vote.

*   *   *

Our boss always said, "When you take this job, you have to make unpopular decisions." Everyone in the office agrees his most unpopular one was taking the job.

The boss asked one employee, "Is there something about me you don't like?" The guy said, "No, it's nothing about you. It's *you* I don't like."

* * *

My boss has a chip on his shoulder . . . right in the spot where everyone else has a head.

♦ You Know Your Boss Hates Your Guts When . . .

. . . everyone else gets a paycheck, but your salary is paid entirely in coins suspended in a mold of gelatin.

* * *

. . . you have to share your office with several brooms, mops, and assorted janitorial supplies.

* * *

. . . your assigned parking space is normally occupied by a trash dumpster.

* * *

. . . on company business trips you usually have to travel as luggage.

* * *

. . . your office has a window in it the same as everyone else's, except that theirs have glass in them.

* * *

. . . you're invited to staff meetings only as a guest of another employee.

* * *

. . . at the company picnic you notice you're the only employee on your side of the rope in the tug-of-war.

* * *

. . . you realize that the office Christmas party is generally scheduled when you take your two-weeks vacation—in July.

... everyone else in the office has an expense account, while you're given a book of coupons for McDonald's Happy Meals®.

* * *

... your annual performance evaluation is not delivered to your personally by your boss, but by two or three semi-professional comedians who work in the area.

* * *

... everyone else flashes an I.D. pass to get by the security guard each morning. You undergo a strip search.

* * *

... the boss bites your head off for every silly little mistake. Not figuratively—literally.

* * *

... at the last seven retirement parties the boss has asked you to fill in for the guest of honor.

* * *

... you realize that three times since you've worked for this person, the company has relocated without telling you where.

* * *

... the only training seminar you've been sent to in the past five years was "How to Write an Effective Letter of Resignation."

* * *

... each time you ask for a raise, instead of giving you a reasonable response, the boss just staples your fingers to the desk.

* * *

... you notice the only time you're asked to work overtime is after bomb scares.

* * *

... yours is the only picture on the organization chart shown both full face and profile.

* * *

... coworkers receive a bonus at the end of the year and you receive a bill.

Newfangled Technology

♦ *Computers*

"Garbage in-garbage out" describes the operation of the computer. In many offices, it also describes the function of the copying machine.

*   *   *

GIGO means "Garbage in-garbage out." Years ago, before computers, that used to define the personnel office.

*   *   *

What did we do before computers? The same as we do now, only not as fast.

. . . And with fewer bugs.

*   *   *

The best thing about a computer is it will do whatever you tell it to do. That's also the worst thing about a computer.

*   *   *

Computers can't think . . . but they're faster than employees who can't think.

. . . And they're less obnoxious than bosses who can't think.

*   *   *

Management likes computers for two reasons: First, they don't come in and ask for a raise every six months. Second, if they did, they'd probably get it.

*   *   *

My boss likes things that work fast. That's why he's partial to computers and prune juice.

*   *   *

The computer doesn't think at all. That's why it doesn't look out of place on my boss's desk.

*   *   *

A computer is a machine that can do things real fast—like get you angry.

If computers ever develop artificial intelligence, how will we tell them apart from some of our coworkers?

* * *

One nice thing about computers is they're turned on first thing in the morning. With employees it usually takes four or five cups of coffee first.

* * *

Computers have drastically changed the business world. Before them, we had to think up excuses for our mistakes.

☞ *TIP #12*

Know the ending of your joke

There is only one reason to tell a joke: The punch line. It's the comedic twist that produces the laugh. It's the heart of the humor.

Everything in an anecdote should point toward the punch line. Everything you say should support the punch line. Nothing should detract from its effectiveness.

Above all, you, the storyteller, should know and fully understand that ending, that punch line. Why? Because it keeps you focused on the humor. It helps you give your listeners enough information to understand the joke, but not go off on tangents that confuse the audience and detract from the effectiveness of the humor.

Knowing the ending and understanding the humor helps you tell your story correctly and effectively.

Let me give you an example:

On a variety show, the host was supposed to have a little exchange with a guest who was the daughter of a famous star. The exchange was supposed to sound like this:

HOST: Wasn't So-and-so your father?

GIRL: He still is.

It was soft, but it was cute. However, it didn't work because the host said:

HOST: *Isn't* So-and-so your father?
All the girl could say was, "Yes."

The effectiveness of the humor was lost because one of the principals either didn't understand or forgot the ending of the joke, the punch line.

◆ *Voice Mail*

I wrote a letter to one company complaining about their voice-mail system. I said, "Please, can't I talk to a rational, logical, thinking, feeling human being?" They wrote back and said, "We don't have any people like that working here."

* * *

You've heard of voice mail . . . that's the "hide-and-go-seek" of the business world.

Voice mail is very convenient. You simply call a person and 23 or 24 confusing button pushes later, you get to talk to him.

. . . Or to his machine.

. . . Or his machine's machine.

* * *

Voice mail is like taking a multiple-choice quiz by telephone.

* * *

Voice-mail proponents say it only takes one finger to push a button. Voice-mail opponents say it only takes one finger to tell you what they think of it, too.

* * *

Some people swear by voice mail; most swear at it.

* * *

Voice mail is confusing to me. By the time I get the person I want, I've forgotten what I wanted him for.

Some companies use voice mail in their service department. That's because by the time the customer finishes pushing button, his warranty runs out.

*   *   *

If Native Americans had had voice mail instead of smoke signals, Custer might be alive today.

*   *   *

If voice mail had been around at the beginning, Alexander Graham Bell might still be trying to find the right buttons to push to reach Watson.

*   *   *

Voice mail is the new executive system for setting up meetings: "Have your machine call my machine."

*   *   *

Voice mail is so prominent nowadays that when some executives call and get a real person, they're offended.

*   *   *

Voice mail can be irritating. According to a recent survey, given a choice, most salmon still prefer swimming upstream to trying to reach their fiancées by voice mail.

*   *   *

We now have machines that answer the phone, machines that dial the phone, machines that call other machines. Do you get the impression the only reason Ma Bell needs us is to pay the bills?

*   *   *

We have voice mail, answering machines, fax machines, automated tellers. If we're not careful, people could become obsolete.

*   *   *

Even the president has installed voice mail on the hot line: "Thank you for calling the White House. If you're considering an all-out nuclear attack on the U.S.A., push one. . . ."

♦ Car Phones

If God thought car phones were absolutely necessary, He wouldn't have created homing pigeons.

* * *

There are two kinds of businesspeople who have car phones—those who need them and those who need to think they need them.

* * *

A car phone is less of a status symbol now than it was a few years ago. Real status nowadays is to be talking to someone on your car phone and say, "Can you hold on a second? My other phone is ringing."

* * *

Everybody should have a car phone. Forget business. The way traffic is nowadays, we need Dial-A-Prayer at our fingertips.

* * *

Telephones on the highways are an improvement over the old communication system—obscene hand signals.

* * *

With one hand on the wheel and one hand on the phone, drivers now have to learn to make obscene gestures with their ears.

* * *

The trouble with a car phone is that once you answer it, you can't tell the caller you're in a meeting.

* * *

Car phones can be dangerous. In an emergency situation you not only have to hit the brakes, but also the hold button.

* * *

Car phones are efficient. You can make a wrong turn and get a wrong number all at the same time.

Cellular phones have made the automobile an extension of the office. You'd be surprised at the number of people driving along the freeways leaning back in the driver's seat with their feet up on the dashboard.

*　*　*

With car phones you can now make business calls on the way to and from work. Just don't try writing off the cost of the freeway as part of your office expenses.

*　*　*

As you drive along the highway now, you notice that most cars have airbags. Some are in the steering wheel and some are on the phone.

*　*　*

Now that so many business people have mobile phones, cold calling has become easier. Just tell the operator, "Connect me to the Pasadena Freeway. I'll talk to anyone."

*　*　*

Businesspeople are progressing in the wrong direction. Rather than being able to make business calls from your car, you should be able to drive your desk to a Las Vegas vacation.

*　*　*

They have phones everywhere now. One gentleman got a call on his car phone. It was for the phone in his briefcase.

☞ *TIP #13*

Tell your story slowly and clearly

Every so often when I'm typing, I'll inadvertently place one hand on the wrong guide keys. I type away at a pretty good clip, then glance up to discover that I've typed jibberish. I've moved my fingers correctly, but they were on the wrong place on the keyboard, so they hit the wrong keys. Instead of "national," I've typed "nsyionsl." The wrong letters are only one key away from the correct ones, but they generate something that can't be read.

Speakers who try humor often make a similar mistake. They find a funny tale that they know will amuse their listeners. They try it out on family and friends and it's a knock-out story. They rehearse it on their own until they have the patter perfected. They tell it a few times in front of an audience and it scores beautifully.

Then they get cocky. For some reason, they feel that good comedy should be fast. The quicker they tell the joke, the "smarter" it will seem. They want to get through all the nonessentials and to that punch line. They want to hear the laughter.

Eventually, they don't hear as much laughter. Why? Because the listeners can't hear the joke. The speaker has speeded up the telling of it so much that the result is jibberish. It's garbled.

A good speaker enunciates all the words, even the ones that are not part of the punch line. Speed doesn't make good humor; timing does.

Take your time. Jack Benny once tried to prove to a beginner that comedians could work slowly. He went onstage and didn't speak. He looked at the audience and did pieces of business until he had to speak. He was in front of the audience getting laughs for seven minutes before he spoke his opening line.

Take your time in telling a joke. Let your audience hear every delightful word.

◆ Beepers

My boss tried to get me to wear a beeper, but I told him I didn't want anything else on my body that might fall off.

My boss said, "Suppose an emergency comes up and I can't find you?" I said, "Call Dial-A-Prayer."

My boss said, "Really important people wear beepers." I said, "No. Really important people have someone else wear the beepers and then come and get them."

My boss said, "That's right. That's why you're wearing a beeper."

* * *

My boss wanted me to wear a beeper. He said, "How else can I summon you when I need you in a hurry?" I said, "Offer a pay increase."

* * *

My boss said, "What's wrong with wearing a beeper? I can reach you anytime I need you." I said, "I think you just answered your own question."

* * *

I hate beepers. If I wanted to live my life that way I would have been born a homing pigeon.

* * *

My boss said, "You should be available at all times of the day or night." I said, "No. I'm just an employee. You've got me confused with the 24-hour virus."

* * *

My boss firmly believes that devoted employees should come anytime they're called. He has us confused with Lassie.

* * *

My boss wants his staff available 24 hours a day. Good management should be authoritative and decisive, but not chronic.

* * *

I hate beepers. The only thing I want around my beltline that goes off unexpectedly is indigestion.

* * *

You've heard of "house arrest"? Wearing a beeper is being under "office arrest."

* * *

Beepers are a terrible invasion of one's privacy. Come to think of it, so is working for somebody else.

Talk about status! My boss is so important he wears a beeper with an unlisted number.

*   *   *

Beepers have a history of going off at the worst times . . . like when you don't want them to.

◆ Copying Machines

Have you ever wondered what we did before duplicating machines? The same thing we do now only without copies.

*   *   *

The rule of thumb in business is: Anything worth doing is worth making 10 or 12 copies of.

*   *   *

Anything in the business world can be easily and cheaply duplicated. Remember that when you go in to demand your next raise.

*   *   *

We had a tough day at the office today. The copying machine broke and we had to get along with one of everything.

*   *   *

Sixty percent of the things run off on our office copying machine have nothing to do with our business, which isn't bad since 75% of the things that happen in our office have nothing to do with our business.

*   *   *

Our boss issued a scathing memo about misusing the copying machine. Then he ran off hundreds of copies and gave them to everyone.

*   *   *

Someone should invent a machine that refuses to copy anything that's silly, useless, and has nothing to do with business. Of course, then we'd have to make carbon copies of all our interoffice memos.

If our office copying machine were used only to make copies of important business documents, we could probably get along without it.

* * *

In the olden days, monks copied all documents by hand. Even then, other monks got them to copy cartoons that they could pass around the monastery.

* * *

Sign over the copying machine: "We're trying not to waste paper. So why'd you write this memo in the first place?"

* * *

Sign over the copying machine: "Remember to remove your original. The machine doesn't want it any more than anyone else does."

* * *

The copy machines are getting very complicated. The new one in our office has a sign on it that reads: "Do not operate without a copilot."

* * *

Our boss will never master the new copier. He still has trouble with the candy machine.

* * *

How come they can make a machine that gives you hundreds of copies for free, but they can't make a vending machine that won't steal your money when you try to buy coffee?

* * *

We have a new copying machine that will enlarge, reduce, collate, staple, print in color, print on both sides, and count pages. Now our office is having trouble trying to generate a document that's important enough to run off on the thing.

* * *

Our new copying machine has so many lights and buttons on it, even if it didn't make copies we would have bought it, anyway—just to amuse the employees.

Timing is listening to your audience

Humor is trickery. It's like stage magic; a good percentage of it is misdirection. An effective joke or humorous story leads an audience in one direction, then suddenly and swiftly changes direction on them.

I liken it also to pulling a rug out from under the listeners. Timing is important. First you have to get them positioned on the rug. Then you have to pull it without warning. If they see it coming, they'll step off.

Timing in telling a humorous joke or story is similar. It's listening to your audience reaction and judging the correct time to "pull the rug out from under them."

The storyteller has to set the audience up for the trick and then quickly spring it on them. You do this by being aware of your audience. As you tell your story, you concentrate more on them than on yourself. You gauge their reaction. You "feel" their response. You judge how long to pause between setup and punch line.

It's a seat-of-the-pants "guesstimate," but it can be done. It can improve with practice. The key to it is to pay attention to your listeners. Listen to them. Let them tell you what to do, and when to do it.

♦ *Fax Machines*

We now have fax machines all over the globe. If the world ended tomorrow, we could continue sending messages until April 23rd.

* * *

Even Dial-A-Prayer now has a fax machine.

* * *

Have you ever seen the cockpit of a 747? That's what the front of our new office fax machine looks like.

Remember the old days when the only thing that had that many buttons on it was the front of a sailor's trousers?

Our new office machine is so elaborate, our employees have trouble generating anything that's important enough to send on it.

* * *

We have machines in the office that do things today that years ago weren't even worth doing.

* * *

We have so many newfangled machines today. The modern office measures productivity in BPS . . . beeps per second.

* * *

In today's office, anything that doesn't beep is turned into a planter.

* * *

How do these machines do all the things they do? I'm still trying to figure out how the drugstore scales could tell my fortune.

* * *

They even have fax dating now. It's dating by telephone. Let your fingers do the flirting.

It's a lot quicker and easier than dating the old-fashioned way—by overnight mail.

* * *

They have fax dating now. It's terrific. You can become a swinger now without ever leaving the house.

If you're promiscuous, you can get a party line.

* * *

Yeah, people swing by the facsimile machine now. It's called "faxomania."

* * *

You can even propose marriage by fax nowadays. The hard part is getting your telephone to get down on one knee.

* * *

It's dangerous dating by fax. How do you know when you've got a bad date, or just a bad connection?

Fax dating can cause problems. Like when you call your one true love and keep getting a busy signal.

And it's caused a new form of male impotence . . . guys who can't get a dial tone.

But it's a very inexpensive date . . . unless you insist on dating out of your area code.

. . . A toll call is true love.

*   *   *

But you have to be careful dating by fax. One gentleman fell in love dating by fax and is now married to an answering machine.

They honeymooned at an AT&T switching station.

The question now is, "How do they bring up the children?"

The marriage may not work out. They're not divorced and they're not separated. She just put him on hold for a while.

. . . He's having a little fling with a cellular phone out in the suburbs.

♦ Vending Machines

When vending machines don't work they hang an "Out of Order" sign on them. They should do that with employees, too.

*   *   *

We have a very elaborate coffee machine. It gives you black coffee, coffee with light or heavy cream, coffee with one sugar, two sugars, or three sugars. It does all those things, but rarely does it remember to give you a cup with it.

It acts just like the government. It takes your money and pours it down the drain.

This one vending machine never makes correct change. It brews your coffee the way you like it, but then it leaves itself a generous tip.

* * *

All the vending machines in our office steal your money. I'm convinced the words "coin operated" are synonymous with "stick 'em up."

* * *

Being a vending machine is a great gimmick. We have a candy machine on the third floor that drives to work each morning in a Mercedes Benz.

* * *

This one machine takes your money and gives you nothing in return. The problem is it's a coffee vending machine, but it thinks it's a piggy bank.

* * *

I went to management and complained. I said, "I'm sick and tired of putting money into something that doesn't work." In response, they showed me my last job evaluation.

* * *

We had a big office celebration at the fourth-floor candy machine last week. It has kept enough money to be promoted from petty theft to grand larceny.

* * *

One vending machine had a sign on it that read "Use exact change only." It didn't want to steal so much money that it moved into a higher tax bracket.

* * *

I put two quarters in one of the vending machines the other day and, boy, did I get a surprise. They work just as good as slugs.

* * *

The first rule of the business world is: Never put money in a vending machine that has heel indentations all up and down the front of it.

One machine in our building gets kicked so much that next to it they put a machine that sells bandages for sprained ankles.

* * *

People punch this machine, kick the machine, and shake the machine because they lose their tempers. But no matter what they do, they also lose their 75 cents.

* * *

Of course, it's silly to curse a machine; it has no emotions. It's silly to kick a machine; it has no feelings. It's silly to argue with a machine; it has no conscience. All it has is your money.

☞ *TIP #15*

Laugh at your own jokes?

Can you laugh at your own jokes? *Should* you laugh at your own jokes? Sure and sure. If you enjoy the humor of your anecdote, you're as entitled to chuckle at it as your listeners are. Is it proper protocol? Is it good showmanship? Again, sure and sure.

It all depends on your style. Look at some of the professionals. Bob Hope rarely laughs at his own material. Jack Benny hardly ever did. Red Skelton giggled at all of his one-liners. It's a matter of delivery.

If it feels natural to you to laugh, laugh. If it doesn't, don't.

The only caveat is that you shouldn't let your own enjoyment of the joke—your own laughter—destroy the enjoyment of the joke for the audience. Don't allow your laughter to interfere with the telling of the story.

Once you've told your anecdote and your listeners are enjoying it, you are welcome to join them. However, laughing while you're telling it or giggling through the anecdote can destroy the rhythm of the humor or can make the story unintelligible to the listeners.

Use some discipline in the telling; but once told, if you enjoy your own joke, laugh along with your audience.

I Love My Coworkers

♦ Secretaries

Do you know why the world is in such terrible shape today? Because God doesn't have a secretary.

God doesn't need a secretary, because He can do all things—even make His own lunch reservations.

* * *

A good secretary knows who the boss is, but lets the boss think he is anyway.

* * *

Secretaries make travel plans, lunch reservations, arrange meetings. They're always telling the boss where to go.

* * *

In the business world, secretaries are the brains behind the people who think they're the brains.

* * *

Good secretaries handle all the filing. They put everything in its place, and occasionally that includes the boss.

* * *

They say if you want something done quickly, give it to a busy man. He'll have his secretary do it.

* * *

An executive without a secretary is like a ship without a rudder—adrift in a sea of undrinkable coffee.

* * *

A secretary is a guardian angel who can type 250 words per minute.

A good secretary can make the boss look so smart that pretty soon even *he* starts to believe it.

* * *

To an executive, a secretary is a safety net who can also make a pretty good first pot of coffee in the morning.

* * *

An executive usually lets the secretary know they're a team that shares responsibilities: "You shoulder the blame, and I'll handle the glory."

* * *

A really good secretary is someone who's worth more than you are but gets paid less.

* * *

Secretaries must be able to tell little white lies like, "He's in a meeting now." Or really big lies like, "He's busy at the moment."

* * *

When a grown man lets go of his mother's apron strings, he reaches out for his secretary's.

♦ Lazy Coworkers

I work with the laziest man alive. He won't even ride the elevator alone. He wants someone else to push the button.

* * *

I work with a man who does absolutely nothing—and does it badly.

* * *

I work with a guy who does so little around the office it may take him 38 years to earn his 25-year pin.

* * *

One coworker of mine makes no bones about being lazy at work. He's shopping around now for a desk that converts to a daybed.

* * *

I work with a guy who is no help to the office team at all. In a tug-of-war, he'd be the rope.

We feel in our office that everyone should do his fair share. This lazy guy agrees . . . almost. He feels that anyone can do *his* share.

*   *   *

I don't mind keeping my nose to the grindstone, but it's keeping my nose to *his* grindstone too that bothers me.

*   *   *

This coworker of mine is the laziest worker in the universe. When the boss calls him into the office he has to meet him halfway.

*   *   *

The only thing this guy has in his "out" basket is dust.

*   *   *

When this lazy coworker of mine retires, I'm going to appropriate his "out" basket. I want to have one that's never been used.

☛ *TIP #16*

Hear your stories as your listeners will hear them

Humor is a seat-of-the-pants skill. It's largely guesswork. Even the professionals—comedians, writers, producers— guess at their material. It's an educated guess, but a guess nonetheless. How can a business speaker predict which material is appropriate for which audience? Which comedy will work? How to deliver the humor most effectively?

Naturally, experience helps, as does the luxury of trying material out beforehand. However, the most helpful tool in evaluating material is to listen to it as your audience will hear it.

Many performers, both professional and business, become self-centered. They see and hear their presentation only from their own viewpoint, their own frame of reference.

It's wise to step out of that role and imagine yourself in the audience. Listen to your material as if you were in the crowd instead of at the podium.

Does it seem funny? Is it apropos? Is it inoffensive? Does it make your point?

Judging material from this vantage point not only broadens your perspective, but gives you a more accurate reading of your material and its potential.

◆ *Absenteeism*

This one guy was absent from work more often than he was there. We always knew when he was coming to work because he'd call the office for directions.

. . . His parking space was the only one that had a victory garden in it.

*   *   *

We had one guy who was out of the office so much, anytime his desk chair was warm, the sprinkler system went off.

*   *   *

We had one worker who missed work regularly. When he'd leave work on Wednesday, he'd wish everybody a pleasant weekend.

*   *   *

We had one worker with a terrible attendance record. He worked in our office for 20 years and was always known as "the new guy."

*   *   *

We had one worker who was a master at avoiding the office. The first time the boss met him was when he presented him with his 25-year pin.

*   *   *

One guy I worked with practically worshiped absenteeism. He had a poster of Amelia Earhart over his desk.

A good day's work is like a mediocre anecdote. . . . "You had to be there."

*　*　*

One worker I know wanted overtime for being absent. He stayed home to rest up and dreamed he was at work.

*　*　*

Then I knew one coworker who was so dim-witted, he could be absent even when he was there.

*　*　*

I knew one worker who hated weekends because it was impossible to be absent from work on those days.

*　*　*

We had one coworker who avoided the office so much we used to mail him his phone messages.

*　*　*

One guy spent so much time out of the office that he was retired for five years before anyone noticed it.

When he died, we all went to his funeral . . . just to see if he would be there.

. . . He was, but it took six guys to carry him there.

◆ Lateness

I work with a gentleman who is late for everything. He rings in the New Year at 12:13.

. . . On January 3rd.

*　*　*

This guy has always been late for everything. His wife's wedding anniversary is three days before his.

*　*　*

This guy has a history of being late. He once got a temporary job playing Santa Claus in a department store. He didn't show up for work until January 6th.

One day the boss asked this employee why he was late for work every single morning. The guy said, "I'm such a good worker, I want to give everybody else a 20-minute head start."

* * *

One guy was late for work every single day of his life, so to get even the company retired him at age 63. It worked perfectly. He left when he was 65.

. . . Of course, he missed the going-away party by three days.

* * *

One day the boss said to this employee, "There are 76 people who work in this office and 75 of them are here on time every day. Why are you always late?" He said, "Because they're the ones who are always cutting me off on the freeway."

* * *

The boss called one employee in and said, "Not only are you always late, but you're getting later and later each day. Why?" The man said, "It takes me longer and longer to think of an excuse I haven't used yet."

* * *

One coworker who was always late had a unique concept to offer his supervisor. He said, "Don't consider me ten minutes late today. Consider me 24 hours and 50 minutes early for tomorrow."

. . . The boss said, "Don't consider yourself fired. Consider yourself retired 33 years and 8 months too early."

* * *

One guy I worked with was always late. The only way you could get to work later than him was to take the day off.

* * *

Once this guy who was always late asked the boss if he could have a half day off work. The boss said, "Which half? The part you're here for, or the part you're late for?"

This guy was late for work so often it took him 16 years to earn his 10-year pin.

. . . Even after he retired, he had to show up for work for 10 minutes a day for 12 years.

* * *

This guy was late for his own funeral. It wasn't his fault, though. All the pallbearers were friends of his, and they were late.

☞ *TIP #17*

Let them know when to laugh

Some professionals boast, "I could read the telephone book and make it sound funny." One comic actually did that on television. He came out and read the phone book. It was crazy; it was bizarre; but was it funny? In a sense it was, but when did you laugh? After the third name? the fourth name? the twenty-fifth name?

As the speaker, the raconteur, your job is to make the people laugh. Consequently, your duty also is to tell them when to laugh. Each of your quotes, one-liners, or anecdotes should have one specific spot where your audience *knows* when to laugh.

When Will Rogers said, "I belong to no organized political party. I'm a Democrat," that last word was the signal to laugh.

Phyllis Diller says, "My husband cut himself shaving this morning. He bled so badly, his eyes cleared up." Everyone knows where the punch line is.

Henny Youngman says, "I went to the doctor with a sore foot. He said he'd have me walking within an hour. He did. He stole my car." That's where you laugh.

Review your own humorous material and be sure that whoever is listening will know exactly when to laugh. Be sure it's clear, it's specific, and it has some punch.

♦ Petty Office Thievery

Our manager once delivered a scathing speech to all his workers on petty thievery—stealing paper clips, pencils, stationery for personal use. When he got back to his office, his desk chair was gone.

*　*　*

We had so much petty theft in our office building that the company put up a sign in the parking lot that read, "Parking—for getaway cars only."

*　*　*

People who work in an office will take anything that they think the company won't notice missing. Last month we had three employees taken.

*　*　*

My boss said he wanted to know about anyone taking anything that didn't actually belong to them. I showed him the list of deductions on my paycheck.

*　*　*

People will stuff anything in their briefcase. Some people call it a briefcase; other people call it an accomplice.

*　*　*

Show me an office worker who doesn't steal office supplies, and I'll show you a person who still hasn't used up what he took last year.

*　*　*

Some people get carried away with stealing office supplies. I worked with one gentleman who has a summer home made completely out of paper clips.

. . . It's stapled to the foundation.

. . . And the exterior is painted completely with marking pens.

*　*　*

Our office started locking the supply cabinet. So far this month, three locks have been stolen.

Our boss said, "Even small, insignificant things in this office still belong to the company." One wag answered, "Good thing, too, or you wouldn't have a job."

* * *

One employee took so many office supplies, rather than try to stop him, the company just asked him to show up for work in a ski mask.

* * *

Some people in our office will take anything that's not glued down. That includes everything, because all the glue was stolen months ago.

* * *

A few of the workers in my office are guilty of petty theft at least once each week—when they accept their paycheck.

* * *

Petty theft of stationery where I worked was so bad that the company had to declare bankruptcy. They had a great financial statement, but they didn't have any paper to print it on.

◆ Annoying Coworkers

One guy I worked with is so boring, his personality was successfully sued by No-Doz®.

* * *

One coworker is so dull, his life once passed before his eyes and he slept through it.

* * *

This guy is so dull, when he goes to the local watering hole after work, happy hour ends.

* * *

This one guy I work with leads such a dull life. One time a gang of us went to a fortune teller. She told our fortunes and gave him his money back.

* * *

This man is boring. Most people change into pajamas before engaging him in conversations.

One guy in our office is so dull, he has to carry a sign that warns: "Do not drive or operate heavy machinery while talking to me."

* * *

There's one guy in our office who loves to argue. He always has. When he was a kid, his first words were, "Oh, yeah!"

* * *

One coworker is very argumentative. He disagrees with everybody—even people who agree with him.

* * *

One guy in our office loves to argue. He can turn "Good morning" into a political debate.

* * *

This one guy in our office has an opinion on every topic . . . and it's always different from everyone else's.

* * *

This gentleman in our office loves to argue. If you say "black," he'll say "white." If you say "night," he'll say "day." If you say, "I agree with you," he'll find someone else to argue with.

* * *

One coworker hums all day. It's like sharing an office with the inside of an elevator.

* * *

One guy in our office hums or sings badly all day long. He can get off key and on your nerves all at the same time.

* * *

Another coworker is so annoying because he's so loud. He thinks louder than I talk.

* * *

One guy in our office has a booming telephone voice. He can leave a message on your phone whether you have an answering machine or not.

* * *

This guy's so loud, his phone was out-of-order for three days before anyone noticed it.

One gentleman who works in our office finds fault with everything. He thinks the alphabet is in the wrong order.

. . . He wants to change it to have the letters listed by height.

. . . Then by experience.

. . . Then by seniority.

♦ Backstabbing

Backstabbing is the art of turning your best friend into your worst enemy without letting him know about it.

* * *

If it were boxing, it would be like hitting your opponent below the belt and blaming it on the referee.

* * *

Backstabbing is what Brutus did to Julius Caesar, thereby starting a corporate fad.

* * *

Backstabbing is the process of turning a friend into a foothold.

* * *

Backstabbing is the business world's way of saying about a coworker: "I've always liked you and I never will."

* * *

Backstabbing is destroying another person so you can move ahead of him. It's fair in love and war. In the business world it's not fair, but it's tolerated.

* * *

Backstabbing is merely climbing up the corporate ladder using former friends in place of rungs.

* * *

Backstabbing is kind of like telling tales out of school and out of context.

* * *

Most backstabbers want success very badly—so that's how they get it.

With backstabbing you find it very difficult to climb the corporate ladder after you've had your legs cut out from under you.

* * *

I won't say we have a lot of backstabbers in our office, but we do have a fax machine, a duplicating machine, and a sharpening stone for imaginary knives.

* * *

We have one person in our office who has never met a vulnerable back he didn't like.

* * *

A backstabber is someone only a mother could love—unless she happens to work in the same office with him.

* * *

Some backstabbers claim that all they're doing is telling the truth about their coworkers, whether it ever happened or not.

* * *

Some coworkers don't backstab. They either have a conscience or don't have an imagination.

☞ *TIP #18*

Have fun with your mistakes

I once watched a speaker totally disintegrate before the audience. He was speaking with some confidence when the microphone in his hands fell apart. It just broke. It wasn't his fault: it was a defective microphone. Nevertheless, it destroyed him.

Even after he got a new microphone he never recovered. His confidence was gone, his concentration evaporated, his message was lost.

He sacrificed his speech for no reason. The minor mishap was easily corrected and didn't disrupt his presentation that much. Besides, the audience understood and was pulling for him. They were sympathetic.

If you make a dumb error at the platform, if something goes wrong, if you tell a joke that doesn't work, have fun with it. Most of the time the audience is on your side. If you play with your mishaps, the listeners will join in the fun.

Some of the most effective humor is self-deprecating. What better chance to have some fun at your own expense than when a few things go wrong? Relax and enjoy your own discomfort. The audience will join you.

◆ Smokers and Nonsmokers

Our office is divided into two sections: the smoking section, and the "wave-your-hand-in-front-of-your-nose-and-make-a-funny-face" section.

* * *

Smoking in the workplace is definitely bad for your health—one of the nonsmokers might kill you.

* * *

In the workplace, smokers and nonsmokers make the Hatfields and the McCoys seem like kissing cousins.

* * *

Our office is divided into smoking and nonsmoking sections. They're clearly separated by the demilitarized zone.

* * *

If looks could kill, smoking in our office would clearly be "injurious to your health."

* * *

Nonsmokers in the workplace are polite, but getting more aggressive. Like this one coworker who said to another, "I'll make you a deal. If you promise to put out that cigarette I'll release you from this chokehold."

One worker asked another, "Do you mind if I smoke?" He replied, "I don't care if you burn."

*   *   *

Smokers can be aggressive, too. One coworker can give up cigarettes anytime he wants, but has discovered now that he's addicted to annoying people.

*   *   *

The smoking/no smoking feud goes on endlessly in the workplace. Every time we try to clear the air, somebody lights up again.

*   *   *

Nonsmokers in our office tried to promote clean air by burning a smoker in effigy.

*   *   *

Smokers in our office demanded a place where they could smoke in peace. The boss suggested the unemployment office.

*   *   *

We had a sign in our office that read, "Thank you for not smoking." Someone set fire to it.

*   *   *

We have a sign in our office that says, "Thank you for not smoking," but it's hard to see it through all the smoke.

*   *   *

We have two signs in our office. One says, "Thank you for not smoking." The other says, "Thank you for not paying any attention to that other sign."

*   *   *

One smoker got so uptight working in a smoke-free atmosphere that he starting biting fingernails . . . anybody's.

Every Office Has 'Em

♦ Office Collections

Two things are certain: death and taxes. Make that three things. After death, somebody always takes up an office collection.

* * *

They take up so many collections where I work, on my income tax form I've listed my job as a business expense.

* * *

They're always taking up a collection in our office. I can't keep my nose to the grindstone because someone is always shoving a cigar box under it.

* * *

One guy in our office loves to take up collections. In fact, his right hand is beginning to get shaped like a cigar box.

* * *

I know a lot of offices take up collections, but ours takes contributions by credit card.

* * *

They take up so many collections at my office that one day I called in sick and they said, "Can you just send in your wallet?"

* * *

Going to my office is like going to church. At least twice a day they take up a collection.

. . . Anytime I put that much money into a collection, I at least expect to get a sermon.

* * *

I've thrown so much money into the pot that by now I think that pot owns a bigger home than I do.

* * *

I donate so much money in the office that I think I'd come out ahead if I just stayed home and joined the Home Shopping Club.

My office is the only place of business I know where you wear out your pants from the pockets first.

* * *

If you forget and leave your money at home, you're officially declared absent.

* * *

Once I told them I left all my money in my other pants. They held these pants as collateral.

* * *

I've given money I didn't have for a coworker I'd never met to buy something he didn't need.

* * *

Once I refused to donate anymore. I said, "I'm sick of all these collections." So they took up a collection for me.

☞ *TIP #19*

Build your own humor file

A fellow comedy writer once told me he had planned to write his own dictionary. However, instead of listing the words alphabetically, he wanted to list them in the order of their importance.

It's a bizarre concept, but it points out one of the obvious benefits of a dictionary—the words are easy to find. If the words were assembled in random order, it would take us forever to find the one we were looking for.

Business speakers have a similar problem when they decide they need a joke, story, or quote to add some humor to a speech they're giving. They have a collection of books on humor, but they now have to search through all of them looking for the joke that will be appropriate. It's a massive task.

I recommend that you begin to assemble your own more manageable, more organized humor file.

First, if you have some books on humor, check off only those items that appeal to you. Circle them, check them off in the margin, or highlight them with colored markers. Then when you do turn to them for reference, you'll cut down your research time considerably.

Second, clip and file items that are usable. You may read a joke that you like in a newspaper or magazine. You may see a cartoon that applies to your work. You may read a quote that impresses you. When you see these items, cut them out and either paste them in a scrapbook or store them in an index card box. Keep them somewhere where you can find them quickly when needed.

Third, make notes of original ideas or stories, jokes, or quotes that you hear, and keep them handy.

Now when you need a touch of humor for a speech, you'll have quick access to material that you've already selected and approved.

◆ Office Rumors

The rule of thumb in our office is that a good rumor is better than nothing to talk about at all.

* * *

You know what a rumor is—it's a fact that management just hasn't thought of yet.

* * *

Speed of light used to be the fastest speed known to man. Now it's the speed of the office rumor.

* * *

One coworker said about an office rumor: "I haven't seen anything spread that fast since Oprah Winfrey went off her diet."

* * *

Rumors spread like wildfire—and both of them create a lot of hot air along the way.

A good rumor is like a truck with bad brakes—neither one of them can be stopped easily.

*   *   *

Office rumors are usually little harbingers of the truth.

*   *   *

Rumors are messengers that are sent on ahead so that reality, when it arrives, won't seem so farfetched.

*   *   *

A rumor is something that you're never quite sure is true or not . . . even if you're the one who started it.

*   *   *

The most annoying part of a good rumor is that by the time you find out whether it's true or not, it's obsolete.

*   *   *

A good rumor has about as much truth in it as a good martini has gin.

*   *   *

That's the trouble with truth—it ruins a lot of interesting rumors.

*   *   *

A good rumor is the missing link between fact and fiction.

*   *   *

We had so many rumors floating around our place of business we had to hire extra people just to listen to them all.

*   *   *

I once started a rumor that I was going to get a big promotion. Management countered with the rumor that it would be for another company.

◆ *The Office Don Juan*

Sex in the office is not a good thing. Sex anyplace where there's a paper shredder is not recommended.

. . . One false move could leave your love life in tatters.

Every office has a Don Juan. You know, a guy who keeps hanging around the copy machine looking for girls who want to reproduce.

* * *

There's usually a Don Juan who uses the workplace instead of a computer dating service.

* * *

The Don Juan in our office is very well known in the business world. His name is written on hundreds of employment applications in the space marked "Reason for leaving your previous employer."

* * *

Our office Don Juan will chase anything wearing a skirt, which we found out when we had a Scottish bagpipe band at one of our company picnics.

* * *

The guy in our office is part Don Juan and part compass. He always points toward the nearest female.

* * *

We call him "the rubber stamp." He wants to date everything that comes into our office.

* * *

Our office Don Juan may someday write the world's shortest book, entitled, "Women I Have Not Tried to Hit On."

* * *

This guy is relentless. To him, the word "no" means "maybe," the word "maybe" means "there's a good chance," and the word "yes" means . . . well, he doesn't know what the word "yes" means. He's never heard it.

* * *

He refuses to take "no" for an answer, although several times he's had to accept it as a court order.

* * *

He thinks he's God's gift to women. If he is, I hope God kept all the receipts.

* * *

He calls himself "The Stud" . . . because no one else will.

All the women in the office call him "G.L.," which is short for "Get Lost."

. . . Some of the women call him "Little Leaguer" because he very rarely gets to first base.

*   *   *

This guy thinks he's entertaining because all the women in the office laugh at him.

Office Fun

♦ *Business Lunches*

I know one executive who takes so long for lunch, every time he comes back he has to fill out an application in the personnel department.

*   *   *

I know one executive who really enjoys long lunches. He gets to his favorite restaurant around 11 A.M. and asks the maître d' for a nice table where he can watch the sunset.

*   *   *

Lunch meeting—that's business jargon for "Somebody mention one of our competitors so we can write this whole thing off."

*   *   *

Some companies routinely put a few drops of vinaigrette dressing on the cover sheet of all their reports. They think it'll help if the IRS ever challenges their business lunch deductions.

*   *   *

Some executives treat lunch exactly the same as being at work. They have a comfortable chair, someone to bring them their coffee, and nothing that happens there is going to be good for their ulcer.

One executive talks business all through his lunches. Once he took his mother out and she said, "Please, dear. It's not polite to speak with your portfolio full."

* * *

My boss has a unique way of ensuring that all of his lunches are business-related. He orders hot soup and cools it off by fanning it with the company's financial report.

* * *

I know one executive who is a gourmet luncher. He never has any food, but he insists on a wine that goes well with five martinis.

* * *

One executive told me he always has light lunches. That means he drinks until the inside of his head feels like the inside of a 125-watt bulb.

* * *

One executive has an hour for lunch so he always orders the same thing—a 55-minute martini and a cab.

* * *

Factory workers have a whistle to signal their lunch hour. Executives have the sound of a cork popping.

* * *

I know one businessperson who does drink a lot at lunch, but he's very status conscious. He always insists that the head waiter give him the best table to be under.

* * *

I know one executive who has well-balanced lunches. He has two drinks for cocktails, two drinks with olives as a main course, and two drinks with cherries in them for dessert.

. . . He doesn't have any coffee, though, because then he'd do nothing but toss and turn all afternoon.

* * *

One executive at lunch said, "I want to have a few drinks to help forget all the work that's piled on my desk." It worked, too. By the end of lunch he couldn't remember which office building his desk was in.

One businessman told his waiter, "I'll have one more martini for the road." The waiter said, "Would you like it straight up?" The man said, "No, I'll have it lying here on the floor like I've had the last three."

* * *

I knew one executive who drank so much during his lunch breaks that for years we thought he had a beard. It was just his breath running down his chin.

◆ Brown Baggers

A brown bagger is a person who packs his lunch before leaving for work in the morning, carries it to the office, stores it in a desk drawer, opens it at lunchtime and eats it, and wonders why with each and every bite.

* * *

Some people "brown bag it" at the office. They're easy to spot. They're the ones who are sober after lunch.

. . . It's hard to carry three martinis in a brown paper bag.

* * *

The people who "brown bag it" are the ones who really should drink at lunch. You should have three martinis before biting into some of those sandwiches.

* * *

One guy looked at his lunch and threw it right in the wastebasket. I said, "Aren't you afraid that'll attract mice?" He said, "Not if they've seen the sandwich."

* * *

Some brown baggers lift the top layer of bread to see what kind of sandwich they have. Then they taste it to see what kind of sandwich they have. After that they have to call home to find out if they were right.

* * *

Don't ever ask a brown bagger what he's having for lunch. He may show it to you and ruin your lunch.

One guy has a surefire way of telling what his sandwich was. He said, "If it's brown, it's cheese. If it's green, it's meat."

* * *

A ham sandwich changes after it's been sitting in a desk drawer for hours with an apple sitting on top of it. It tastes like a slice of pool-table felt between two slices of Play-Doh®.

* * *

I saw one coworker who had a brown bag with a red line around it. I asked what that was for. He said, "When the grease stain rises above that line, I throw it out."

* * *

One guy threw his lunch away because it was the fourth time in a row he had a tuna sandwich. The really sad part is that he packs his own lunch.

* * *

Some people "brown bag it" because it's faster, some because it's cheaper, others because they just happen to like food that's been sitting in a desk drawer for four to five hours.

* * *

The good thing about bringing lunch in a brown bag is that you can eat it during the morning and then go out and have lunch anyway.

* * *

We had one guy in our office who brought his own lunch in a brown paper bag every single day for 13 years. We called him "Ptomaine Tony."

* * *

One guy's wife always packed a note with his lunch that said, "I love you." I told him I thought that was nice. He said: "If she really loved me, she'd eat these sandwiches."

Research your own material

Whenever my brothers and sisters gather together, we retell favorite family stories and laugh at them as if we were hearing them for the first time. When I meet people I used to work with, we relive stories that invariably begin with "Hey, remember the time that . . ."

Each of us has a wealth of anecdotes in our mental archives. These are stories that are worthwhile because they've stayed alive in people's memories for so long. And these stories are *real*.

Often these stories, like wine, improve with age. Various storytellers add embellishments, perhaps bend the truth a bit to make them more interesting or amusing. That's all right. These tales are entertainment, not historical documentation.

You might spend some leisure time recalling some of your own past history. Jot down the stories that you tell and hear when you're with family, friends, or coworkers. You may get much entertaining and educational material that could go into your presentations.

◆ *The Office Party*

The motto of the office party is: "Eat, drink, and be merry, for tomorrow the boss may remember what you said."

*   *   *

Stay sober at all office parties. It's better to go to sleep not having any fun than to wake up not having any job.

*   *   *

Keep cool at all office parties. Some employees with short fuses discover they work for people with long memories.

*   *   *

Keep this in mind at the office party: If you tell the boss how you hate working for him tonight, he may tell you that you're not working for him tomorrow.

If you get too loose at the office party, you may say some things you wish you hadn't said—and management may agree with that.

* * *

A good rule of thumb for all office parties is: It's all right to drink like a fish provided you drink what a fish drinks.

* * *

Keep your mouth shut at all office parties. It's easier to keep your foot out of it that way.

* * *

The office party is when you can lose your inhibitions and your job simultaneously.

* * *

Be nice to everybody at the office party. It's hard to tell the chiefs from the Indians when all their faces are blurry.

* * *

The office party is like being arrested—anything you say can and will be used against you.

* * *

The best way to get through an office party unscathed is to glue your tongue to the roof of your mouth.

. . . It not only keeps you quiet, but it keeps you from overindulging in the cheese dip.

. . . And no one will notice because after an hour they'll all be talking like you anyway.

* * *

Remember this about the office party: When someone says, "You can speak freely," you know it's going to cost you.

* * *

Good advice for any office party: Keep your mouth shut and your options open.

* * *

You know you've acted unwisely at the office party if . . .

. . . when you go to leave, your manager tells you to take all your personal belongings with you.

. . . you show up for work the next morning and your desk is the only one with yellow police tape around it.

* * *

. . . you show up for work the next day and all your co-workers introduce you to their lawyers.

* * *

. . . when you arrive at work the next morning, your assigned parking space is surrounded by irate husbands.

* * *

. . . you punch the time clock the next morning, and it punches you back.

* * *

. . . you arrive at work the next day and discover a gallows being erected where your desk used to be.

* * *

. . . when you arrive at the office the following morning, you discover that your photo in the organizational chart has a black border around it.

* * *

. . . when you arrive at the staff meeting the following day, you notice that your chair is in the corner facing the wall.

* * *

. . . you arrive at work the following morning, sit in your chair, put your feet up on your desk, and then realize that you haven't gone into the building yet.

* * *

. . . you arrive at work the next day and learn that the company has moved and left no forwarding address.

♦ Briefcases

If there were no such thing as the business world, some briefcase salesman would have invented it.

* * *

Briefcase—that's a security blanket with a handle.

If a businessman were on a sinking ship and all he could save were either his briefcase or his wife, which would he throw overboard? It's a hypothetical question, but all spouses should learn to swim.

* * *

Businessmen love their briefcases. Oh, they look like they're just carrying them, but it's really fondling.

* * *

I know one businessman who always has a briefcase in his hand—even when his hand is in his pocket.

* * *

There's a word for a businessman who's not carrying a briefcase—lackadaisical.

* * *

To some businessmen it's more than a briefcase—it's a pet.

I know one who even taught his briefcase to "stay."

* * *

A good businessman and his briefcase are a team. As soon as a businessman sits down in an airplane, his briefcase pops open.

* * *

Have you ever noticed on an airplane, when an executive opens his briefcase, how packed it is? Some rooms in my home have less in them than that.

* * *

Some executives have more in their briefcases than they have in their job descriptions.

* * *

Some of those briefcases are so packed, it's hard to tell whether these guys are going to a business meeting or on a camping trip.

* * *

I don't know what all some businessmen carry in their briefcases, but I wish I had that much put away for my kids.

Some executives pack so much into their briefcases, when they open them, they look like portable attics.

*   *   *

One guy I know packs everything into his briefcase except his secretary.

If they ever come out with laptop secretaries, he'll hire one and put it in there, too.

☛ *TIP #21*

Use proven humor

Bishop Fulton J. Sheen had a highly rated television show in the early '50s. He claimed he was successful because he had good writers—Matthew, Mark, Luke, and John.

In your business speaking, you can employ some of the top comedy minds in the business. You can use humor that has stood the test of time. You can use one-liners that are proven laugh-getters.

If you're warning your audience against foolhardy moves, you might tell them that "there are two times in a man's life when he should not speculate: when he can afford it and when he can't." You might also tell them that Mark Twain said it first.

If you're advising managers, you might quote Samuel Goldwyn, who said: "I don't want any yes-men around me. I want everybody to tell me the truth even if it costs them their jobs."

If you're discussing clarity in verbal and written communications, you might cite an example from Casey Stengel, who told his players at spring training to "stand in alphabetical order according to height."

All you need is a good book of quotations, or better yet, a book of humorous quotations. When you want to illustrate a point with a touch of humor, read through and pick out one you like. It's in there because it's time-tested.

As Christian N. Bovee said: "Next to being witty myself, the best thing is to quote another's wit."

◆ Things You'll Seldom Overhear Around the Watercooler

"I love my boss so much I'd gladly work for him for free."

* * *

"I'm going to run down to the cafeteria and ask the cook down there for one of his recipes."

* * *

"To me, 'The customer is always right' is not just a saying; it's a way of life."

* * *

"Well, we've finally got the thermostat set in our office where everybody is happy with the temperature."

* * *

"Boy, I wish I could make coffee as good as that vending machine on the third floor."

* * *

"I wish they'd find more for me to do. I'm starting to get bored around here."

* * *

"The boss wanted to give me a raise but I said, 'Let's wait until I really deserve it.' "

* * *

"I'm sure the boss knew I was only kidding about all those things you said at the company picnic."

* * *

"Don't you just love Monday mornings?"

* * *

"I don't want the promotion if it's going to make my coworkers envious."

* * *

"I don't want this ever to happen again—that you take up an office collection and forget to ask me to contribute."

"I don't really want to know who you saw the boss coming out of that sleazy motel with."

* * *

"Yes, I've heard that nasty rumor, but I don't believe it."

* * *

"I love the parking space I've been assigned. It's equidistant from my home and the office."

* * *

"They wanted to give me an office with a window but I said, 'No, it would only be a distraction.' "

* * *

"So the boss says to me, 'Don't worry about profit. We're just interested in turning out a good product.' "

* * *

"Charlie never does any of the work, but he's always there to grab the glory. It's a pleasure to work with someone so resourceful."

* * *

"My vacation was nice, but I'd much rather be here with my coworkers."

* * *

"I work here for the satisfaction, not the money."

* * *

"What? Is it quitting time already?"

Fasten Your Seat Belt

♦ Business Travel

Travel is the scourge of the business world. I knew one guy who traveled so much that eventually he wouldn't even park in his own driveway. He thought it was for loading and unloading only.

I know one businessman who spent so much time away from home, his children used to get him confused with the guy who read the gas meter.

. . . He began to suspect that his wife did, too.

* * *

One guy I know went four weeks straight without business travel. He got so disoriented that he lost his own luggage.

* * *

One businessperson I know spent so much time in airports he put four Hare Krishnas through college.

* * *

Years ago, the words "You're going places" meant you had some potential in the company. Nowadays, it's a job description.

* * *

One businessperson has accumulated so many frequent flyer miles, when his boss finally tells him to go to hell, the trip will be free.

* * *

One guy travelled so much for his company he developed a bad back. His spine kept trying to return to its fully upright and locked position.

* * *

One businessman did so much travelling he said he was actually looking forward to his own funeral. It was the only trip he could go on without worrying about losing his luggage.

* * *

One businessperson traveled extensively for his company. He said he had been to almost as many places as his luggage had.

* * *

It's a sad situation when your luggage builds up more frequent flyer mileage than you do.

One company issued cost-saving travel rules: No one travels first class; upper management travels coach; all others travel either in the overhead compartment or under the seat in front of them.

* * *

One company uses such a low-cost airline that, instead of movies for in-flight entertainment, they play hide-and-go-seek.

* * *

One airline asked me what sort of special meal I wanted prepared. I said, "Edible."

* * *

Do you know why some people consider it safer to sit in the back of the plane? Because there's a better chance the airline will run out of meals before they get there.

◆ Hotels and Motels

Our company books the cheapest hotel accommodations. I stayed in one room that was so small, if you ordered room service, they delivered it to the room next door.

* * *

One room the company booked for me was so small, when the bellhop carried my bags in, there was no room for me.

* * *

One room was so small it came with a Murphy bed. If you wanted to lie down, you had to open the bed and the window.

* * *

This room was so tiny, I ordered a pizza from room service. They had to deliver it one slice at a time.

* * *

I stayed in one room that was so tiny, I opened my copy of *Playboy* and set off the sprinkler system.

One room I stayed in was so small, I called the manager to complain about how cold the room was. He came up and put a larger bulb in the lamp.

* * *

I stayed in one hotel room that was so small when you opened the closet door the room disappeared.

* * *

This room was so small if you had food delivered to your room, you had to eat it from the hallway.

* * *

The company has put me in hotels where I hated to get off the elevator. It was larger than my room.

* * *

In one hotel, the walls were so thin I could hear the couple next door just thinking about making love.

* * *

The walls were so thin in one hotel, when they guy next door made hand shadows on the wall, I applauded.

* * *

I've stayed in motels where the walls were so thin you could hear people talking in the next room. This was the first time I could tell if they had bad breath or not.

* * *

One motel I stayed at, the walls were so thin I could always tell when the guy next door had a woman in his room. I could smell her perfume.

* * *

One place the company put me up at had the thinnest walls I've ever seen. I could follow the conversation of the people in the next room . . . and they were using sign language.

* * *

The company has booked me in some pretty crummy dives. At once place, I plugged in my electric razor and all the television sets in the place went off.

How to make a story your own

Many of the stories that humorists tell aren't their own. They're researched from joke collections, magazines, public domain. Practically every anecdote that Abraham Lincoln told could be traced back to its source. Yet, once Lincoln told it, it became a "Lincoln story." You can accomplish the same proprietorship by making each story you tell *your* story, regardless of where you get your humorous anecdotes. You do this by surrounding it with truth—truth that applies to you.

For instance, if you're telling a story about a child, make it your son or daughter, your niece or your nephew. If you're telling a story about a golfer, make it one of the people at the head table or one of the guys you play with regularly at your club.

Even if you tell a story about some famous person—a story that could not possibly be about you—you can still make it apply to you by telling how you heard it or where you read it.

A story that begins "I was having a drink with the president of this association one night . . ." is better than a story that starts "These two guys came into a bar . . ."

Work a bit on your humor presentation to make it apply to you or your audience.

♦ *Conventions*

A convention is a three-day hangover at which you install the officers for the coming year.

* * *

People drink a lot at business conventions. The most common injury at most conventions is frostbite of the fingertips on the glass-holding hand.

Here's a gentleman who's unclear on the concept. While packing for a convention he asked his wife, "Which tie do you think goes better with a party hat?"

*　　*　　*

One company I worked for understood that business people did a lot of drinking at the annual convention. On the convention report form, the name of the city was a multiple-choice question.

. . . So was the name of the person filing the report.

*　　*　　*

People do drink too much at conventions. That's why the Red Cross Bloodmobile never shows up until at least one month after the annual convention.

*　　*　　*

One CEO stood up at the opening session and said, "All of you spent too much time at the hospitality suite last night. I can tell because your faces are all fuzzy this morning."

*　　*　　*

One company found a way to increase attendance at the convention breakfast meetings. They held them at three o'clock in the afternoon.

. . . All the non-golfers attended.

*　　*　　*

One conventioneer complained that someone stole his wallet right out of his pants pocket. The boss asked who did it. The man said, "How would I know? I wasn't in the same room as my pants at the time."

*　　*　　*

Conventions serve a useful purpose. If it weren't for them, the boss might not win a golf tournament all year long.

*　　*　　*

Conventions are the time for the three G's—golf, guzzling, and "Geez, does anybody remember what room I'm in?"

One conventioneer said, "There's one thing I wish I could remember—what my room number is." Another convention-eer tried to help and asked, "What's your name?" He said, "Okay, that's *two* things I wish I could remember."

*   *   *

Most conventions have a golf tournament where your handicap is the party the night before.

*   *   *

Clubs know when they're hosting a convention golf tour-nament. They have a sign that says, "Please replace all divots, repair all ball marks, and remove all swizzle sticks."

◆ *Expense Accounts*

Many expense accounts are a collection of little white lies with decimal points in them.

*   *   *

For some, the expense account is just a convenient way of giving yourself a bonus without even troubling the company.

*   *   *

Many business travellers think the expense account is the means by which the company reimburses you for money you've spent, whether you've spent it or not.

*   *   *

Docudramas are a style of writing that combines fact with fiction. Expense accounts are another.

*   *   *

Some business travellers think the expense account is the business world's way of saying, "And be sure to keep a little something for yourself, too."

*   *   *

A rule of thumb is to be as honest on your expense account as you are on your golf score card.

*   *   *

Expense accounts are there to make business travellers feel secure. No matter how far you roam, you can still reach into the company's pocket.

Some business people just try to be efficient. They figure they can take a client to lunch and the company to the cleaners all at the same time.

* * *

Some companies, no matter what you turn in on your expense account, it comes back disapproved. And they're not shy about it, either. Their official expense account forms are printed in the shape of a boomerang.

* * *

One company I worked for disapproved about 60% of all expenses submitted. I hardly made a profit at all.

* * *

Some companies are very frugal with their expense money. I asked one, "How do you want me to travel—as a first class or a coach passenger?" They said, "As a flight attendant."

* * *

One company balked at my expense report. They said, "You made a hefty profit on this recent business trip. How about rewriting your expense account and sharing some of it with the company?"

* * *

One company told an employee, "We think the expenses you turned in are a little exorbitant, but we're going to approve payment anyway. Consider it your severance pay."

* * *

One of my bosses put it rather succinctly. He said, "I'll leave the decision entirely up to you. You can either have what you asked for on your expense account or your job back."

☛ *TIP #23*

Hit your audience right between the eyes

Once I was travelling on a military trip with Bob Hope doing wartime shows for the service personnel. We were scheduled to land in the Azores, but the pilot warned us that heavy winds might prevent our landing. Hope said to me, "Write some wind jokes."

I did. However, it was too dangerous to attempt a landing, so we flew on to Spain. Hope came down the aisle again, gave the wind jokes back to me and said, "Do some Spain jokes."

I did, and that night they played like gangbusters.

Bob Hope always wanted material that was tailored to *this particular audience*. He knew that good jokes played better when they hit listeners right between the eyes. People like jokes about themselves.

Take extra effort to guarantee that your humor applies to your listeners. The closer it comes to them, to their location, to their unique situation, the more it will be appreciated by them.

Take the Money and Run

◆ *Payday*

Payday makes it all worthwhile . . . before taxes.

* * *

Payday is when you open your envelope and find out what a pound of flesh is going for these days.

* * *

Is payday your reward for a job well done last week, or just a way to dupe you into coming back to work again next week?

* * *

The most distressing part of payday is that most companies insist on paying us what we're worth.

* * *

"A fair day's pay for a fair day's work" seems workable in theory. Usually, though, both employer and employee are disgruntled with it.

They say a penny saved is a penny earned. Wouldn't it be nice if a penny earned were a penny saved?

* * *

Payday is nice. It's one of the few days of the month when you go to bed richer than you woke up.

* * *

Remember how the Seven Dwarfs used to sing, "We work all day and get no pay?" Why do I suspect that was a tax dodge?

* * *

They call it "take home" pay because it won't pay your carfare to anyplace else.

* * *

Researchers say most people don't work for the money. I wish those researchers would introduce me to those people. I'll take their share.

◆ Payroll Deductions

Anyone who thinks leeches are no longer used hasn't seen the deductions taken out of my paycheck each week.

* * *

At the end of the year when the government says, "Who are your dependents?" I say, "You are."

* * *

I work hard because I've got a lot of mouths to feed . . . and some of these mouths I've never even met.

* * *

We all love payroll deductions . . . like a rosebush loves aphids.

* * *

Do you know why they call it "take home pay"? Because after all the deductions, you're ashamed to be seen with it in public.

* * *

They say that too many cooks can spoil the broth. I know that too many deductions can sure louse up a paycheck.

All these deductions are listed on the paycheck stub with a lot of fancy-sounding initials. Put them all together, they spell "mooch."

*   *   *

If all these people share in my paycheck, how come I'm the only one who has to get out of bed when the alarm clock rings?

*   *   *

Sometimes it's hard to tell which is receding faster—my hairline or my take-home pay.

*   *   *

Someone should invent the "Take Home Pay Diet." No matter what you eat, a portion of the calories goes to some government agency.

*   *   *

My payroll deductions finally maxxed out. All I get now is a receipt and 10 to 12 thank-you notes.

*   *   *

Years ago people used to work hard to make both ends meet. With all the payroll deductions today, most of us can't afford two ends.

*   *   *

There was so little left in my last paycheck that the company cashier asked, "Do you want that to go?"

*   *   *

It seems like there are more and more deductions. We used to get a regular paycheck; now we get "paycheck lite."

*   *   *

Our paycheck seems to shrink more and more. The secret is to get a job where the salary is Sanforized®.

♦ You Know It's Time to Ask for a Raise When . . .

. . . your son has a baseball card worth more than your weekly take-home pay.

. . . the supermarket checkout clerk giggles every time you try to cash your paycheck.

* * *

. . . the IRS mails back your tax return with a note reading, "What happened to the rest of your income?"

* * *

. . . you realize you're not only working like a dog, but also being paid like one.

* * *

. . . you give your children a decent allowance and it amounts to a 50-50 split of your take-home pay.

* * *

. . . after your last pay raise you sent a nice thank-you note to President Nixon.

* * *

. . . you discover the company isn't going to fire you because putting an ad in the paper costs more than keeping you.

* * *

. . . you've given up trying to keep pace with the cost of living. Now you're just trying to keep abreast of the cost of surviving.

* * *

. . . after several years on the job you discover you've worked your way up to an entry-level position.

* * *

. . . you realize you have nothing to lose. You make almost as much if they fire you as if they keep you.

☛ *TIP #24*

Don't announce your jokes

Writers have a saying: "Put it on paper." That's a warning against those writers who build up their stories, their scripts with high praise—often praise that's so magnified it can't be justified. "If it's that good," we say, "put it on paper."

The same is true for speakers who are adding jokes, quotes, or anecdotes to their presentations. They don't need to be announced. They don't require justification. They don't have to presented with promises of greatness.

If they're good, telling them is enough.

"Here's a funny story that I know you're going to love."

"This is probably the greatest line I ever heard in my life."

"This will have you falling down laughing . . . I promise."

These are not only unnecessary, they are harmful to the humor. First, they warn the audience that a joke is coming. Humor is most effective when it's a surprise. Second, they build expectations to such a high degree, you can't deliver. Third, they slightly offend a listening audience. The people who hear you want to reserve the right to judge your presentation. It's rude to tell them what they will or won't like.

Resist the urge to glorify your anecdote unless it's totally a part of the telling of it. Get to your story quickly, tell it efficiently, deliver the punch line, and let the audience enjoy it.

◆ Budgets

Budget: That's a Latin word meaning, "Whatever you need, you can't have."

* * *

Every business executive is given a budget—no money, just a budget.

* * *

A budget is the business world's way of saying: "We want you to manufacture silk purses, but we can only allow you so many sow's ears to get you started."

* * *

It's a known scientific fact that you can't make something from nothing. So the business world invented the budget, which means you have to make something from next to nothing.

The business philosophy is that anything that's worth doing is worth doing for less.

*   *   *

In the business world you have to justify every dollar you spend. It's what separates it from government.

*   *   *

A budget is just a way of keeping track of money you don't have.

*   *   *

To upper management a budget means: "We're not going to give you any money, but we expect you to keep track of it."

*   *   *

Budget time is when you tell management, "Here's what I need"; management tells you, "Here's what we can afford"; and the figure you settle on is somewhere below both.

*   *   *

Budget time is when management won't give you the money to do what you told them couldn't be done in the first place.

Get Me Outta Here

♦ Job-Related Stress

Stress is nature's way of saying, "Watch me tie a sheepshank knot with your stomach."

*   *   *

Stress is your stomach saying to you, "Tell your boss to go to hell so I can digest a meal for a change."

*   *   *

There was one job applicant who was so stressed out from his last job, under "hobbies" he listed "teeth gnashing."

Sometimes a little stress can help you lose weight. It's hard to eat too much when you can't get your teeth unclenched.

*   *   *

Stress is getting to you when you notice that you hate to go to work in the morning, and your wife and kids hate to see you come home from work at night.

*   *   *

You know the stress is overwhelming you when you have two martinis for lunch and you tell the bartender to hold the gin and add Maalox®.

*   *   *

You know you're stressed out when you get home from work at the end of the day to find that your wife has hired someone to ask, "How was work, Honey?"

*   *   *

Job-related stress has defeated you when you notice that ambition in your life has been replaced by antacids.

*   *   *

A good way to quiet stress is to laugh at your troubles. If you find you can't stop laughing, you're having a nervous breakdown.

*   *   *

You know your stress is reaching a dangerous level when the only thing that people say to you at work is: "Come in off that ledge."

◆ You Know You Hate Your Job When . . .

. . . you have your morning coffee with two lumps—not of sugar, of Maalox®.

*   *   *

. . . the only way you can stay there for the required eight hours a day is to put a couple drops of Super Glue® on your desk chair.

*   *   *

. . . you can tell how close you're getting to the office by how loudly you're gnashing your teeth.

. . . the only way you can get yourself to the office in the morning is by using a cattle prod on yourself.

* * *

. . . you've volunteered for early retirement even though you're only 33 years old.

* * *

. . . your response to the first person in the office who says "Good morning" is to hit him in the mouth with your briefcase.

* * *

. . . you've been reprimanded several times for running through the corridors naked shouting, "Thank God it's Friday . . . Thank God it's Friday."

* * *

. . . you wish you were born identical twins so that you could take turns and only have to go to work every other day.

* * *

. . . you're caught tampering with the controls of the self-service elevators so they'll refuse to stop at the floor where you work.

* * *

. . . you not only use an alarm clock to get you out of bed in the morning, but also a team of wild horses.

* * *

. . . you purposely go to work through the toughest parts of town in hopes that you'll be mugged and rendered unconscious, thereby having to skip a day or two of work.

* * *

. . . your ulcers get so active that they frequently set off the office sprinkler system.

* * *

. . . you've been reprimanded several times because your weeping and wailing is bothering the other employees.

* * *

. . . you're seriously considering taking up arson as a hobby.

. . . you ask your manager if the company has a parole policy or time off for good behavior.

☞ *TIP #25*

Don't do what you can't do

Not every vocalist can sing every song. Not every juggler can do every trick. Not everyone can tell every joke.

I saw one young comedian do a routine in a comedy club that was a serious philosophical and political debate between William Buckley Jr. and Elmer Fudd. It was hilarious . . . but only when told by someone who could do the voices of Buckley and Fudd.

If you can't do those impressions, don't attempt that material.

Some jokes depend on dialect. If you do that dialect well, you can tell those jokes. If you can't do the dialect, you can't tell those jokes.

Some jokes depend on loud, angry inflections. Some depend on gestures. Some depend on funny faces. Be sure you can do whatever the joke needs. If you can't, don't tell the joke. It's as simple as that.

How do you decide? Try the jokes. Honestly evaluate your own performance. Tell them to your friends and ask their opinions.

Remember that just because you heard someone else tell the joke and get laughs with it, that doesn't mean that you can tell it, too. If you can, fine. If you can't, find another story to tell.

♦ *T.G.I.F.*

Friday is not the most beautiful day of the week. It's just a warning signal that the two most beautiful days of the week are coming up.

Friday is a sign that not only all good things must come to an end, but all bad things, too.

* * *

Friday is the carriage return on the typewriter of life.

* * *

Friday is the one-minute rest between rounds in a boxing match. Even if you're losing because of a TKO, it still feels good.

* * *

Friday is not an ending, it's a joyous beginning. It's like saying goodbye to your in-laws at the airport.

* * *

Friday is an extra-special day. You stopped thinking about work sometime around Wednesday, but on Friday you can also stop doing it.

* * *

It's Friday—you're another week closer to retirement and another week closer to needing it.

* * *

We work for five days and rest two. God worked for six days and rested one. He should've joined the union.

* * *

Friday marks the end of five days of frustration, fatigue, incompetence, and disillusionment—and tomorrow you play golf.

* * *

The only good thing about Mondays, Tuesdays, Wednesday, and Thursdays is that they're prerequisites to Fridays.

* * *

We're grateful that God made Friday. Sometimes we just get a little annoyed that He put it so far back in the week.

* * *

Thank God it's Friday. Tomorrow you can sleep as late as your kids will let you.

Thank God it's Friday. Tomorrow you don't work; you spend time with your family. Tomorrow you don't have to do whatever you're told; just whatever you're asked.

* * *

Thank God it's Friday. Tomorrow you can do things around the house that you've been wanting to do all week—like sleep.

* * *

The drive home from work is different on Friday evenings. Other motorists still make obscene gestures, but they're smiling while they're doing it.

♦ Vacation

Vacation is a time when we look forward to refreshing peace and quiet away from the chaotic workplace, and some solitude. And then the family ruins it by wanting to come along.

* * *

I like to take a vacation to get away from it all, then I wind up tying "it all" on the top of my station wagon and taking it with me.

* * *

Vacation is a time to leave the office behind. And the way my wife and kids pack, that's about all we leave behind.

* * *

For me, vacation is a time to pack the kids in the car and visit all the restrooms on the highways of America.

* * *

Vacation is a time when we're supposed to get away and forget. At least, that's what I told my wife when we got to the airport and discovered that I didn't bring the tickets.

* * *

Vacation is a chance to get away from the hectic rat race, only to find that 75% of the rats take their vacation the same time and place that you do.

All vacation spots are basically the same—a swimming pool completely surrounded by gift shops.

* * *

The best days of any two-week vacation are the first three days. Those are the ones you can afford.

* * *

Isn't it amazing that we have to work 50 weeks a year to be able to afford a decent two-week vacation?

* * *

You know that credit card ad that says "Don't leave home without it"? I have news for them: You *can't* leave home without it.

* * *

A vacation is a way of going places you've never been, to do things you don't like with people you've never met and with money you don't have.

* * *

I sent postcards to all my friends while I was on vacation. I wrote: "Wish you were here, because I certainly can't afford it."

* * *

You know what vacation is? It's liposuction of the wallet.

* * *

Vacations are magical. You go away and come back; your money just goes away.

* * *

A clerk at one hotel said, "You should leave all your valuables in the hotel safe." I said, "I've already been on vacation one week. I don't have any more valuables."

* * *

But everybody should get away for a little while. After all, mosquitoes have to eat, too.

* * *

On my vacation I played a lot of golf and did a lot of fishing. Now I'm anxious to get back to work. I want to start telling the truth again.

I went to a very nice golf resort on my vacation. I want to go back there next year and try playing the fairways.

* * *

I don't understand it. I went on a two-week vacation. When I got back to the office there were four weeks of phone calls waiting for me.

* * *

When I got back from vacation my desk was piled high with unfinished work waiting to be done. Next time I go on vacation, I'm taking the desk with me.

☞ *TIP #26*

Where do the jokes go?

Humor in a business speech can serve to illustrate or reinforce a salient point, or it can just serve to refresh and rejuvenate your listeners.

If it's there to complement part of your message, then it should be near that part of the message. It can come immediately before or immediately after it, wherever it feels the most effective.

Sometimes it's nice to tell a story that entertains and then explain what you were trying to illustrate with that tale. Other times it's more beneficial to make your point and then corroborate it with an illustrative story or quote.

It's a seat-of-the-pants call that's up to your judgment.

If your humor is meant to refresh your audience, then you have to spot when their attention is lagging and lift their spirits with an amusing anecdote.

In either case, you'll find that appropriate humor used in the correct spot can strengthen your presentation.

◆ *Retirement*

Retirement: the only form of doing nothing that you don't have to be elected to.

Retirement means you can finally do whatever you want, only it comes at a time when you don't feel like doing it anymore.

* * *

One bad feature of retirement is that you never have a day off to look forward to.

* * *

Some people retire to fish and play golf and find out they're as bad at those things as they were at working.

* * *

There is a bad feature of retirement: Who do you go to to ask for a raise?

* * *

Retirement is twice the free time with half the pay.

* * *

Retirement is stress management carried to the extreme.

* * *

Retirement is the rest you've earned when you're too tired to enjoy it.

* * *

Some people hate retirement because it means doing nothing all day. It reminds them too much of work.

* * *

The nice part of retirement is that when you get out of bed in the morning, that's the most work you'll have to do all day.

* * *

The secret of a happy retirement is to find something interesting to do, and then not do it.

* * *

A retiree can sit and rock all day on the porch if he wants to. And any retiree who gives that up to go back to work is off his rocker.

* * *

Retirement is great. You can not only do anything you want, but at a senior-citizen discount.

Retirement is beautiful. You can do nothing any time you want to, and even follow it up with a nap.

*　*　*

Retirement is when you can finally do all those things you've always wanted to do. The hard part now is remembering what they were.

◆ *Pink Slips*

My boss promised me a little something extra in my pay envelope. It was a pink slip.

*　*　*

You know what a pink slip is—that's a "Dear John" letter from the personnel department.

. . . It politely takes back your key to the executive washroom by saying, "Be a dear and don't use our john anymore."

*　*　*

A pink slip is the company's way of saying "We don't know what we'd ever do without you, but starting next week we're going to find out."

*　*　*

A pink slip is like a kiss on both cheeks from a corporate Don Corleone.

*　*　*

"Pink slip" is how you spell "employee" in the past tense.

*　*　*

A pink slip is management's way of saying, "We know how you hate to come to work, so don't bother doing it anymore.

. . . At least not here, anyway."

*　*　*

They call it a pink slip because that's the color of the wound it leaves on your ego.

*　*　*

Being pink-slipped is an awful experience. You get a terribly empty feeling in the pit of your wallet.

It's cruel. The company says, "Here's two weeks' pay. Try to make it last the rest of your life."

* * *

When my boss handed me a pink slip he said, "Don't worry. You'll bounce back." Just what I needed—bungee-jumping lessons from the guy who just fired me.

* * *

Our company at least had pink slips that told the truth: "We love your work, but we hate your guts."

* * *

I look on the bright side of the pink slip—at last I got a decent parking space in front of my own house.

. . . And I'll have it for as long as I can keep up the payments.

☞ *TIP #27*

Humor to avoid

There are some forms of humor that don't belong in the business speaker's repertoire. They may be used occasionally, but there are risks. If you don't know what you're doing with them, it might be better to avoid them. Here are some:
Slapstick or physical humor: It usually comes off looking undignified.

Gratuitous insults: Insult humor can often be used effectively, but you must be careful. However, insults that are not founded on any kind of spirit of fun are always dangerous. Insulting for the sake of insulting is not humor.

Put-down humor: These are the kinds of jokes that imply "I'm better than you, and don't you forget it." They can antagonize an audience. It's much better to pick on yourself than your listeners.

Sarcasm: Avoid lines that are disguised as wit but are really vindictiveness. Listeners usually see through the pretense.

Questionable taste: This covers dirty jokes, ethnic humor, hurtful humor, and a few other areas. The humor you use reflects your taste just as the clothes you wear. It's never worth offending anyone with your wit. The best rule is: "If in doubt, leave it out."

Humor that contradicts your philosophy: As a business-person you have a philosophy and a set of ethics that you adhere to. Your humor should be consistent with that. More than a few politicians have found that what they say in jest can be harmful to their careers. Even your jokes should reflect your beliefs.

Index

ability to tell jokes, 34
absenteeism, 75–76
acceptances
of good introductions, 14–15
and fee, 15
gracious, 15
and self-perception, 15
and speech, 15
of speech by someone who doesn't know speaker, 15
of playfully bad introductions, 15–16
and chance, 16
disappointing, 16
and speaker's recommendations, 16
airbags, 62
airline meals, 102
alarm clock, 18, 111, 116
Alcoholics Anonymous, 36
Allen, Woody, 38
annoying coworkers, 80–82
argumentative coworker, 81
loud coworker, 81
Apostles, 12
audience work, 11
beepers, 63–65
Bell, Alexander Graham, 60
Benny, Jack, 63, 71
best man, 54
boss hates you, 55–56
and business trips, 55
and Christmas party, 55
and company picnic, 55

boss hates you (cont.)
and location of parking space, 55
and window in office, 55
Bovee, Christian N., 100
brain, 46
briefcases, 30, 62, 79, 97–99
brown baggers, 93–94
Buckley, William Jr., 117
budgets, 10, 113–114
burlesque, 41
Bush, George, 10
business ethics, 32
business lunches, 91–93
business travel, 98, 101–103
candy machine, 66
car phones, 61–62
carpooling, 22
cellular phones, 61
cheap boss, 51–52
chicken, 18
Christmas, 19, 52, 55
cigarette, 22
clients, 33–34, 52, 108
Clinton, Bill, 10
clown, 41
coffee, 18, 25, 26–27, 36, 52, 66, 69, 70, 72, 73, 91, 92, 100
and facing the boss, 26
and Final Exit, 26
and NASA, 26
cold calling, 62
collections, 100
committees, 35
and lunch, 35
commuting, 21–22
company picnic, 54, 55, 100
computers, 57–58

confidence, 83
conventions, 105–107
copying machines, 57, 65–66, 90
Corleone, Don, 123
Cosby, Bill, 38
coworkers, 26, 40, 56, 58, 76, 82, 87, 100
credit card, 32, 86, 120
Custer, Gen., 60
customers, 33–34
Dangerfield, Rodney, 37, 41
dank office, 29
day of rest, 20
days of week, 19, 100, 116, 117–119
deadlines, 39, 40
death, 36
deficit, 10
Democrat, 20, 78
desktop, 24
Dial-A-Prayer, 61, 63, 67
dignified humor, 20
Diller, Phyllis, 78
dirty jokes, 124
doctors, 33
Don Juan, 89–91
Douglas, Stephen, 11
dreary office, 29
driver's license, 23
due dates, 39
Earhart, Amelia, 75
early bird, 17, 22
Einstein, Albert, 46
elevator, 81
ethnic humor, 124
expense accounts, 52, 56, 107–108
fathers, 17, 20
fax machines, 32, 67–69, 83
fax dating, 68–69
filing, 28–29

Final Exit, 26
firing squad, 18
forgetful boss, 49–51
frequent flyer miles, 52,
    102
Friday, 19, 116, 117–
    119
fringe benefit, 24
Fudd, Elmer, 117
gestures, 16
God, 32, 39, 61, 72, 90,
    117–119
going-away party, 77
Golden Rule, 32
Goldwyn, Samuel, 99
Gone With the Wind,
    29
Gore, Al, 10
grandfather, 18
grandmother, 18
gratuitous insults, 124
grouchy boss, 47–48
Grumpy, 18
Hackett, Buddy, 41
hangover, 105
Hare Krishna, 102
hated job, 115–117
Hatfields, 84
hidden agenda, 23
highway, 21, 22
Home Shopping Club,
    86
honesty in business,
    32–33
Hooker, General Joe, 20
hookers, 33
Hope, Bob, 20, 108–
    109
hotels, 103–104
humility, 28
humor and memory, 12,
    24
humor file, 87–88
humor as enticement to
    listening, 11, 35
hurry, 21
husbands, 97
Hyde, Mr., 19

I.D. passes, 42–43
imaginary friend, 54
introductions
    deserving speakers,
        13
    flowery, 14
    inviting speakers, 13
    none needed, 14
    playful, 13
    recommended speak-
        ers, 13
    simple, 14
    speakers who need no,
        13
    truthful, 13
    undeserving, 13
IRS, 91, 112
Jekyll, Dr., 19
John, 99
Julius Ceasar, 82
Kennedy, John, 10
Krazy Glue®, 51
Lassie, 64
lateness, 76–78
lawyers, 32, 52, 97
lazy coworker, 73–74,
    101
Lewis, Richard, 41
Lincoln, Abraham, 11,
    105
Livingstone, David, 24
Luke, 99
lunch, 51, 52, 72, 91–
    94, 108, 115
    and committees, 35
    and meetings, 36
    and office size, 31
Maalox®, 27, 115
Ma Bell, 60
map, 17
Mark, 99
Matthew, 99
McCoys, 84
meetings
    and car phones, 61
    and coffee, 36
    and lunch, 36
memos, 38–39, 65

Mercedes Benz, 70
messy desk
    and boss, 25
    and coffee, 25
    and health, 25
    and lost items, 25
mistakes, 83
Monday, 19, 20, 100,
    118
morning, 17
motels, 103–104
Muzak®, 30
naps, 18
NASA, 26
Nixon, Richard, 20,
    112
No-Doz®, 80
office collections, 86–87,
    100
office party, 95–97
    bad moves at, 96–97
office
    and briefcase, 30
    and broom closet, 55
office supplies, 79
O'Hara, Scarlett, 35
open-mindedness, 28
paperwork, buried, 24
parking lot, 30
parking space, 75, 100
    distance of space from
        office, 22–23
    great, 23
    and office size, 30,
        31
    and performance re-
        view, 23
    and pink slip, 124
    and relationship to
        boss, 55
    and status, 22–23
Pasadena Freeway, 62
passport, 23
paycheck, 79, 80, 110–
    111
payday, 20, 109–110
payments
    on car, 21

payroll deductions, 110–111
performance review, 23
Perot, Ross, 10
personnel office, 57, 91
physical humor, 124
pink slips, 123–124
Pinkerton Detective Agency, 42
Play-Doh®, 94
preparedness, 28
presidents
  Bush, George, 10
  Clinton, Bill, 10
  Kennedy, John, 20
  Lincoln, Abraham, 11, 105
  Nixon, Richard, 20, 112
pugilism, 20
purpose, 23
put-down humor, 124
Quayle, Dan, 10
questionable taste, 124
relaxation, 24
research, 95
respect of audience, 16
retirement, 24, 56, 76, 121–123
Rivers, Joan, 37
Rogers, Will, 20, 78
rumors, 88–89, 101
salary, 40
  raise, 56, 57, 64, 65, 111–112, 122
Santa Claus, 76
sarcasm, 124
Saturday, 19
scheduling, 39–40
secretaries, 72–73
  and briefcase, 99
  and coffee, 27, 52
  and filing system, 28–29
  and food taster, 54
  and messy desk, 25

secretaries (cont.)
  and parking space, 23
  security, 42–43
  seeing red, 19
Seven Dwarfs, 18, 110
severance pay, 108
sex, 89
Shakespeare, William, 49
Sheen, Bishop Fulton J., 99
shoplifters, 32
shower, 18
Skelton, Red, 71
slapstick, 124
sleeping, 17
smokers and nonsmokers, 84–85
  aggressive smokers, 85
spouse, 22, 76, 94, 97, 98, 102, 106, 115, 119
sprinkler system, 75, 103, 116
Stanley, H. M., 24
status, 23, 24
Stengel, Casey, 99
Stockdale, Jim, 10
stress, 21, 114–115
stupid boss, 45–47
suggestion box, 43–44
suicide hot line, 54
Sunday, 19
Super Glue®, 115
suspenders, 49
T.G.I.F., 116, 117–119
tax audit, 14
taxes, 86, 109, 110
technology, 57–71
  beepers, 63–65
    unlisted number, 65
  car phones, 61–62
  cellular phones, 61
  computers, 57–58
  copying machines, 57, 65–66, 90

technology (cont.)
  fax machines, 67–69, 83
    fax dating, 68–69
  vending machines, 69–71
  voice mail, 59–60
telephone, 25
Ten Commandments, 32
thievery, 79–80
Thursday, 19, 118
timing, 67
traffic, 21, 22
travel, 98
Tuesday, 19, 118
Twain, Mark, 99
undertakers, 33
unemployment office, 85
unlikable boss, 54
vacation, 62, 101, 119–121
vending machines, 69–71, 100
voice mail, 59–60
waking up, 17
Wall Street Journal, 45
wallet, 51, 86, 106, 120, 123
watercooler, 30, 100
Watson, Mr., 60
Wednesday, 19, 118
weekend, 19, 117–119
White House, 60
wife, 22, 76, 94, 98, 102, 106, 115, 119
Williams, Robin, 41
window, 55, 101
windowless office, 29
Winfrey, Oprah, 88
Wisdom, 11
wit, 11
work at home, 21
"you" "more", 37
Youngman, Henny, 78
Zzyzzenflaus, Mr., 23